Homemade Healthy Dog Food Cookbook

Guide & Cookbook with 100+ Delicious, Easy & Fast Recipes to Feed your Furry Best Friend. Nutritious Tasty Meals & Treats for Everyday to Keep your Dog Happy & Healthy

Lisa Carter

This book is dedicated to:

_____

© COPYRIGHT 2024:
LISA CARTER - ALL RIGHTS RESERVED

The content contained within this book may not be reproduced, duplicated, or transmitted without direct written permission from the author or the publisher.

Under no circumstances will any blame or legal responsibility be held against the publisher, or author, for any damages, reparation, or monetary loss due to the information contained within this book, either directly or indirectly.

Legal Notice:

This book is copyright-protected. It is only for personal use. You cannot amend, distribute, sell, use, quote, or paraphrase any part, or the content within this book, without the author's or publisher's consent.

Disclaimer Notice:

Please note the information contained within this document is for educational and entertainment purposes only. All effort has been executed to present accurate, up-to-date, reliable, and complete information. No warranties of any kind are declared or implied. Readers acknowledge that the author is not engaged in the rendering of legal, financial, medical, or professional advice. The content within this book has been derived from various sources. Please consult a licensed professional before attempting any techniques outlined in this book.

By reading this document, the reader agrees that under no circumstances is the author responsible for any losses, direct or indirect, that are incurred as a result of the use of the information contained within this document, including, but not limited to, errors, omissions, or inaccuracies.

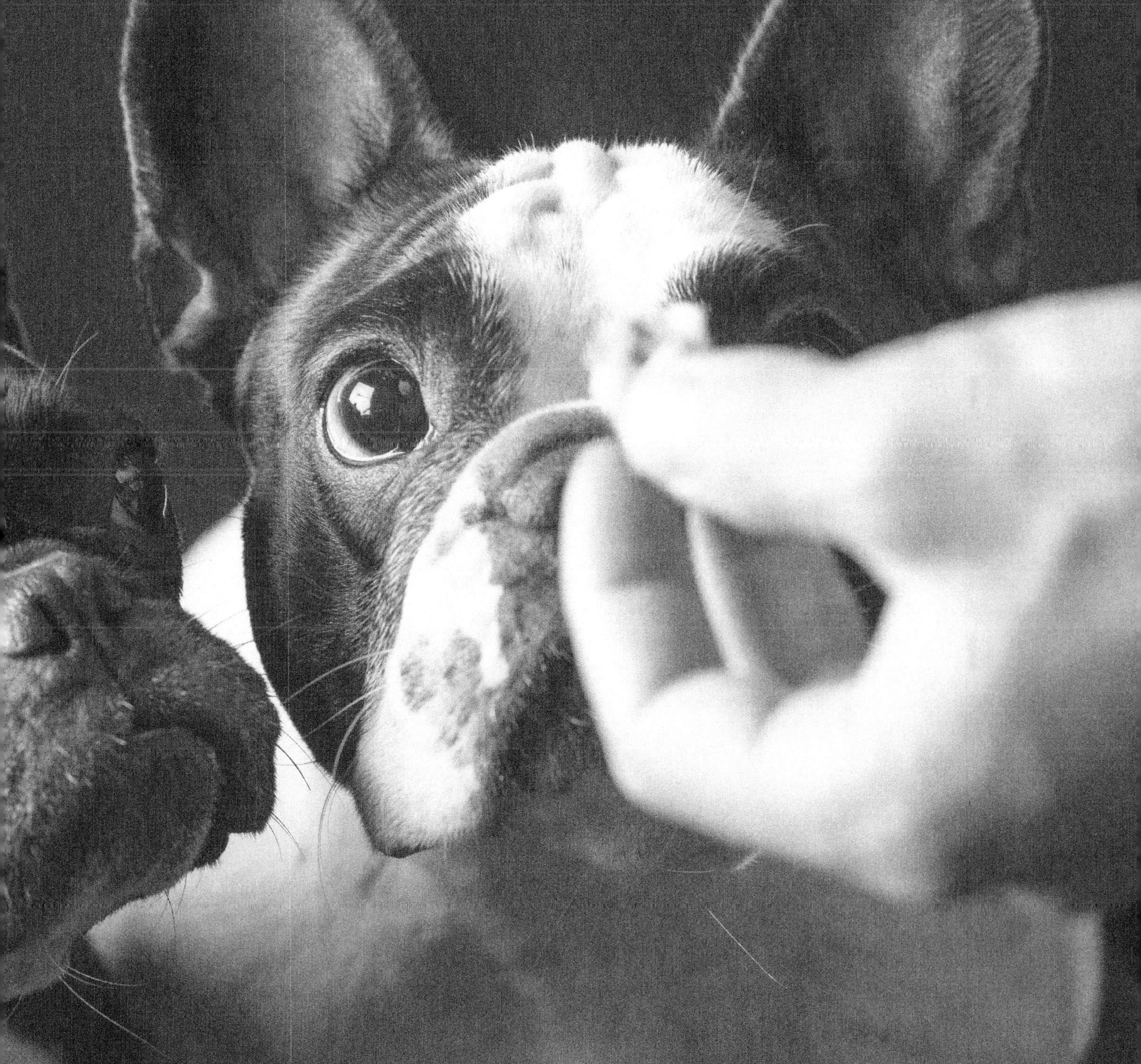

TABLE OF CONTENTS

Introduction 13
    What Is a Homemade Dog Food Diet 13
    Benefits of Natural or Organic Food 15
    Being in Control of The Ingredients and Quality Of Your Dog's Food 15
    Types of Homemade Dog Food Diets 16
    Transitioning From Store-Bought Food to Homemade 17

Chapter 1
Benefits of Homemade Food for Dogs 19
    Benefits of Homemade Dog Food 19
    Cons of Homemade Dog Food 20

Chapter 2
Common Mistakes and Foods to AVOID 23
    Common Mistakes with Homemade Dog Food 23
    What Foods Should Your Dog Never Eat? 24

Chapter 3
Nutritional Guidelines 27
    Proteins 28
    Carbohydrates 29
    Soluble Fiber 29
    Fats 30
    Water Requirements 30
    Vitamins 31
    Minerals 32
    Allergies 35
    How much Should My Dog Eat? 35

Chapter 4
Supplements to Be Used to Optimize Diet 39

Chapter 5
Preparations, Tools, and Storage of Dog Food 41
    Preparing Homemade Dog Food 41
    Making Canned Dog Food 46

Appliances and Tools 46

How to Store Homemade Dog Food 48

Chapter 6
100 Recipes 53

Basic Recipes 53

   1 South Pacific Hot Dogs 54

   2 Pampered Pooch Rice and Lamb Casserole 55

   3 Stomach Friendly Kibble 56

   4 Chuck and Barley Stew 57

   5 Rice With Beef and Fish 58

BakedRecipes 59

   6 Bacon Gravy 60

   7 Cheese Biscuits 61

   8 Crunchy Apple Cupcakes 62

   9 Doggie Bagels 63

   10 Liver Gravy 64

   11 Doggy Cookies 65

No-Bake Recipes 66

   12 Raw Veggie Cupcakes 67

   13 Raw Veggie and Fruit Treat 68

   14 Tuna Casserole 69

   15 Dehydrated Sweet Potato Chews 70

   16 Tapioca and Tofu 71

Breakfast Recipes 72

   17 Spinach Omelet 73

   18 Homemade Breakfast for Dogs 74

   19 Liver Corn Bread 75

   20 Cheesy Eggs and Rice 76

   21 Homemade Dog French Omelet 77

   22 Peanut Butter Oatmeal 78

   23 Pumpkin & Berry Oatmeal 79

   24 Cottage Cheese Breakfast 80

   25 Baked Eggs Muffins 81

   26 Chia Seed Oatmeal 82

   27 Fishermen's Eggs 83

Beef Based Recipes 84

   28 Turmeric Beef 85

   29 Ground Meat Loaf 86

30 Beef and Sweet Potato Stew 87
31 Ground Beef Homestyle Dinner 88
32 Cabbage Beefy salad 89
33 Beef Fried Rice 90
34 Beef Stew 91

Fish Based Recipes 92
35 Parsley Fish & Oregano 93
36 Rice and Salmon 94
37 Vegetable/Fish Patties 95
38 Fish Homestyle Dinner 96
39 Salmon Balls 97
40 Salmon and Spinach Hash 98
41 Appetizing Sea Food 99
42 Tuna Balls 100

ChickenBasedRecipes 101
43 Homemade Chicken Broth 102
44 Chicken Risotto 103
45 Basic Chicken With Rice 104
46 Chicken Casserole 105
47 Poultry Palooza 106
48 Chicken Thighs and Tabbouleh 107
49 Chicken and Cheese Meal 108
50 Chicken and Vegetable Medley 109
51 Turkey Gravy 110
52 Turkey and Vegetables 111
53 Chicken & Sweet Potato 112

Slowcooker Recipes 113
54 Easy Slow Beef and Beans 114
55 Slow Beef and Turkey 115
56 Slow-Cooked Chicken and Barley 116
57 Slow Chicken 117
58 Brothsicles 118

Pastries & Special Occasion Recipes 119
59 Valentine's Day Red Bell Pepper Cookies 120
60 Birthday Blueberry Cupcakes 121
61 Birthday Bones 122
62 Valentine Hearts 123
63 Sweet Potato Potstickers 124

64 Potato Cranberry Christmas Cookies ... 125
65 Halloween Chicken Fingers ... 126

Recipes for Senior Dogs ... 127
66 Senior Dogs Chili ... 128
67 Chicken Cookies ... 129
68 Beef Dinner Delight ... 130
69 Senior Chicken Dinner ... 131
70 Bean Soup ... 132
71 Fruity Chicken Soup ... 133
72 Max and Penny's Spinach ... 134
73 Chickpea Stew ... 135
74 Pumpkin Balls ... 136
75 Pumpkin Rice ... 137

Sweet Treats ... 138
76 Pumpkin-Apple Dog Treats ... 139
77 Quick and Easy Homemade Dog Treat ... 140
78 Peanut Butter and Banana Dog Biscuits ... 141
79 Almond and Banana Treats ... 142
80 Carob Dog Biscuits ... 143
81 Basic Baked Chicken Treats ... 144
82 Apple Cheddar Biscuits ... 145
83 Peanut Butter Treats ... 146
84 Pumpkin Treats ... 147

Training Treats ... 148
85 Homemade Dog Treats ... 149
86 Kale Chips ... 150
87 Sparky's Doggie Treats ... 151
88 Banana and Sunflower Dog Cookies ... 152
89 Chia Carrot Treats ... 153

Frozen Treats for Hot Days ... 154
90 Creamy Yogurt Dog Pops ... 155
91 Peanut Butter & Jelly Frozen Pops ... 156
92 Frozen Fall Pumpkin Treats ... 157
93 Dog Ice Cream ... 158
94 Frozen King KONG® ... 159
95 Frosty Paws ... 160
96 Pumpkin Ice Cream ... 161
97 Banana Ice Cubes ... 162

- 98 Caribbean Canine Coolers 163
- 99 Fido's Frozen Fruit Pupsicles 164
- 100 Peanut Butter and Banana Dog Ice Cream 165

Dental Treats 166
- 101 Homemade Sunflower Dog Treats 167
- 102 Chicken Jerky 168
- 103 Bacon Treats 169
- 104 Pumpkin Turmeric Treats 170
- 105 Liver Logs 171

Chapter 7
Shopping List 173
- Shopping List for Your Dog 173

Chapter 8
Conversion Tables 177

Index 179

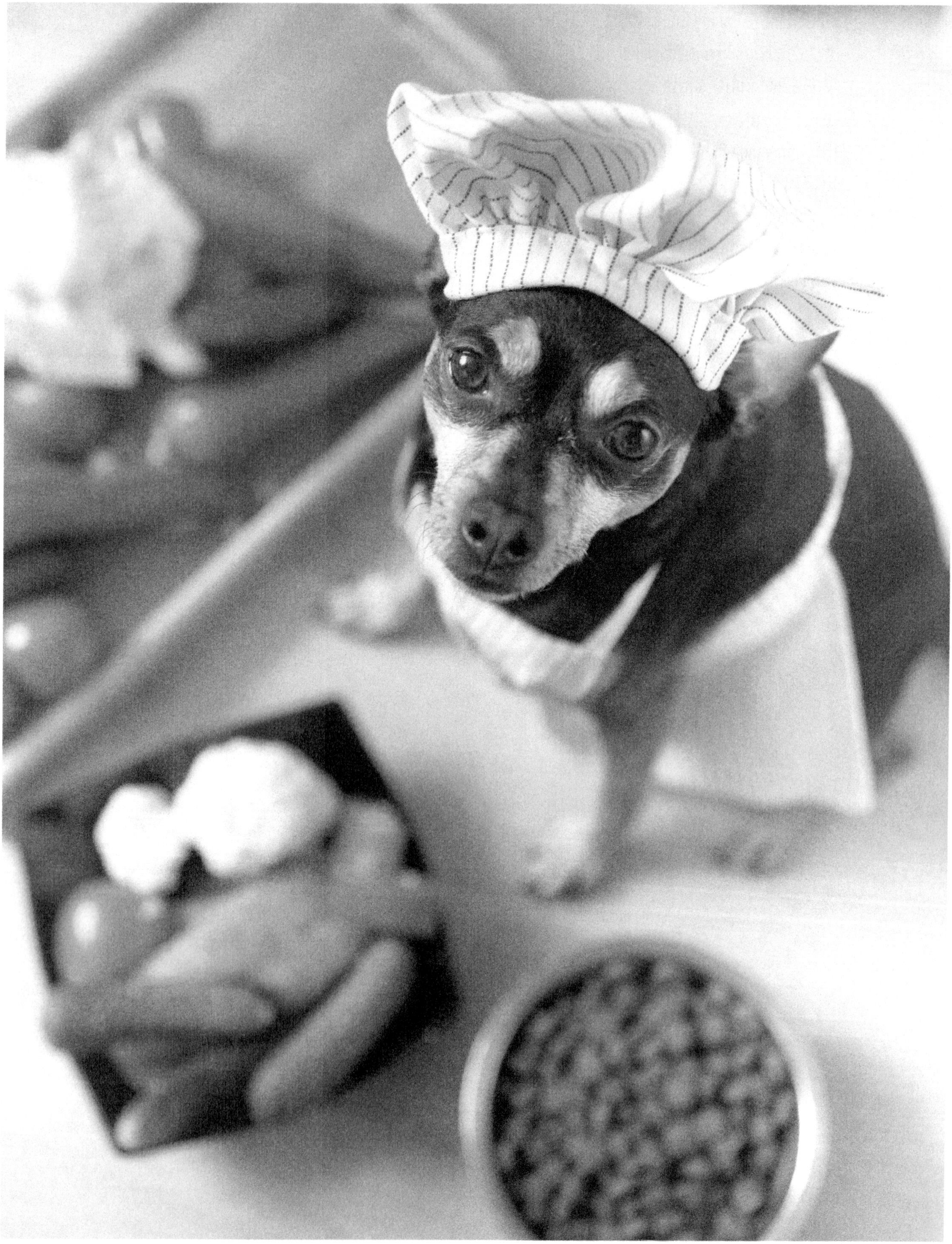

INTRODUCTION

Purchasing and preparing your food almost always results in higher-quality meals. When you do this, you'll always know where your meat comes from and how fresh it is.

This book will review some of the advantages of making your dog food! Then we'll give you recipes for making your dog food and treats for your four-legged friend.

What Is a Homemade Dog Food Diet

Your dog will reap all of these incredible benefits if the homemade dog food is properly prepared and nutritionally balanced. You can't or shouldn't always believe what's on the label.

When it comes to feeding your small dog, it's critical that you understand his nutritional requirements, but know what to give to your puppy and what not to give, and how to ensure he's getting a well-balanced and healthy diet.

Homemade dog food is food prepared and cooked at home for your pets using the same human food ingredients that you would use in your diet. A pet fed a homemade diet is less likely to consume processed commercial foods like dry kibble, dehydrated food, or canned wet food.

People may choose to prepare their pet food for various reasons. Consider whether any of the following apply to you:

- Concerns about commercial pet food recall.
- Animals in need of medical attention.
- Meals that are appealing to picky eaters.
- Pets who are allergic to a variety of food ingredients.
- Wanting to improve the quality of ingredients or the food-making process's quality control.
- Knowing what ingredients are in each meal, you feed your pet.

Recently, there has been much more debate about the commercial pet food industry. There have been nearly constant recalls and diet trends, both good and bad. This is why more people are avoiding commercial pet food and opting for a homemade option to provide their pets with a healthy alternative. However, preparing a homemade meal for your pet is a little more complicated than simply combining ingredients. Following that, we'll look at the different types of homemade diets you can make for your pet.

Consider your diet. You may eat certain foods or recipes regularly, but you vary them to avoid boredom and malnutrition. For example, beef jerky is tasty, but would you want to eat it every meal? Dry dog food sold in stores is dehydrated, baked, and condensed, removing all moisture content. Does this sound familiar? It's the same as drying out beef jerky.

When you cook for your dog, you know exactly what is going into its body. This makes it easier to identify potential issues and adjust ingredients to meet their specific nutritional requirements. Mass-produced dog food typically contains a long list of ingredients, including preservatives, making it difficult to determine which are beneficial to your dog and which are harmful.

There will be no more running out of dog food and having to rush out to the pet store before they close now that you've decided to become a home chef for your dog. You'll still need to go grocery shopping, but chances are you're already doing so. Another significant benefit? The fresh and frozen ingredients in these recipes will add a lot of moisture to your dog's meals when cooked. This is a great way to ensure that your buddy gets enough water every day. Dogs can become dehydrated if they do not drink enough water. Your dog is likely to frequent the water bowl on days with long hikes, hot weather, or high activity. Aside from these days, the average dog sleeps 12 to 14 hours per day, so trips to the watering hole may be less frequent than they should be.

Home-cooked meals are just another way to provide the best for them. Don't be concerned if cooking for your dog sounds like a lot of work. Just like preparing meals for yourself or your family, you'll quickly get into a routine and be able to whip up simple recipes with minimal effort. Once you've determined which ingredients are boosting your dog's performance, you can modify other recipes in the book to include more powerful ingredients. The recipes are intended to give you the flexibility to incorporate cooking for your dog into your life in the way that works best for you.

All dogs must consume the proper food to preserve their health and well-being by ingesting a variety of vitamins and minerals. It's also crucial to keep an eye on a small dog's food because many smaller breeds, especially indoor dogs who may not receive much activity, are prone to weight gain, which can negatively impact their health in a variety of ways. When it comes to feeding your little dog a nutritious diet, some crucial considerations are as follows:

1. Regularly feed your puppy:

Unless your veterinarian or breeder advises differently, most small puppies require food in little doses several times per day. The portions can increase as the puppy gets older and the dog can eat twice daily.

2. Purchase high-quality food:

While it may be tempting to choose less expensive canned and dried foods, doing so will not benefit your dog. Cheaper, lower-quality kibble and canned food contain far fewer nutrients, depriving your dog of essential vitamins and minerals. Because lower quality food lacks nutrients, he will feel hungry and will eat more of it to feel satisfied, which could result in a long-term cost to you equal to that of higher quality food.

3. Combine canned and kibble food:

Kibble should be included in some of your dog's meals to help maintain his dental health. Because many small dogs are prone to oral problems, this could be an important part of their diet. You can feed your dog an entirely dry diet rather than canned food since there are so many high-quality "complete" dried foods available for dogs these days. Complete dried formulas provide all of your dog's vitamins and nutrients while also promoting good dental and overall health.

4. Control treat portions:

It can be all too easy to give your small dog more food without giving it much thought when he looks up at you with those lovely eyes and then looks down at his empty dish, even if he may have eaten an hour ago. You must be careful not to overfeed your dog because many little dogs are prone to weight gain. Make sure to give him precisely measured servings, and be mindful of how many goodies you give him in between meals.

5. Exercise:

Depending on your small dog breed, you should be sure to mix healthy food for your dog with a productive exercise routine. He will stay fit and healthy if he exercises regularly, even if it is simply a little exercise like playing in the garden.

6. Water:

You are responsible for ensuring your small dog or puppy always has access to clean water.

The real question is whether making your dog food at home benefits a man's best friend. While many people claim it is better, there is no scientific evidence to back it up. Myths about what constitutes quality ingredients frequently influence this notion. While there is no scientific evidence that homemade diets have specific benefits, we do know that whole-food-based diets are better over time. Commercial dog foods are meant to be complete and balanced but are not very appealing.

When it comes to variety, providing whole food options makes sense. As previously stated, there are numerous reasons why you might want to make your pet food. The most important of these reasons is gaining control over your pet's diet. So, let's take a look at some of the advantages of making your pet food.

Benefits of Natural or Organic Food

I believe that a natural or organic diet is extremely beneficial to both animals and humans. Artificial flavors, colors, and additives can cause health problems, including allergies. Not only for your pets but also for yourself. Why should any of us consume something synthetic? Artificial ingredients aren't natural; they're created in laboratories and aren't always safe.

A natural or organic diet will have the greatest impact on your dog's health and nutritional intake. Unfortunately, a natural and organic diet can be costly. In the long run, it appears that doctor bills are far more expensive, but that is just my opinion.

Much of what I'm saying may seem repetitive. Your pet's health and well-being should be prioritized, as the risks can be fatal. Commercialized pet food has some advantages, but the risks outweigh the advantages. Feeding your dog as close to a natural and organic diet as possible may add years to their life while also increasing the value of their time with us.

The fillers used in any food, whether for humans or animals, appear to leave us hungry. Natural and organic foods do not contain fillers, so your dog will consume less. It is the nourishment that they truly require. When I first started feeding my dogs homemade food and treats, they seemed to go a little overboard because it was so tasty. A bowl of homemade food goes further because it contains all of the necessary nutrients.

By-products are also used in pet food, as well as human food (just saying). Things like hooves and chicken feet are cooked down or ground up and added to pet food. Sure, they can eat those things, but they definitely shouldn't be something they consume daily. Some foods are difficult to digest, which can lead to bellyaches and, even worse, blockages in their intestines.

Being in Control of The Ingredients and Quality Of Your Dog's Food

One of the best benefits of making homemade dog food is that you have complete control over what your dog eats. You have complete control over the ingredients used in your dog's food. You are preparing healthy canine cuisine for your dog by selecting fresh ingredients and preparing them in a healthy and tasty way that your best friend will truly enjoy and appreciate.

Making homemade dog food is an excellent way to express affection for your special four-legged family member. Controlling your dog's diet will cause you to become much more actively invested in his nutritional health and well-being, taking extra care to select quality foods to include in his daily diet.

You can select fruits and vegetables during their high season when they will be less expensive and more nutritious. Fresh fruits and vegetables are an excellent source of nutrition for your dog. Although your dog's digestive system cannot break down the cellulose walls in raw plant cells, they can still benefit from these nutritious foods when cooked or broken down using kitchen utensils such as a blender, food processor, or juicer. The nutrients in nutrient-rich fruits and vegetables are bioavailable to your dog after you purée, cook, steam, or juice them.

Brightly colored fruits and vegetables are high in nutrients for both you and your canine companion. Some of my favorite ingredients to include in Wallace's dog meals are as follows:

Carrots: Carrots are a popular snack for many dogs, and they can be chewed raw as an alternative to rawhide. To give your dog the many nutrients that a carrot can provide, you must first cook, purée, or steam the carrot to release the vitamins it contains.

Sweet potatoes are a great chew, or you can purée them and add them to a meal for your dog that is high in vitamin B6, vitamin C, beta carotene, and other nutrients.

Peanut butter: Most dogs adore peanut butter, which is high in protein, healthy fats, and vitamins. If possible, use organic peanut butter with no added sugar.

Bananas: Dogs love bananas; simply add a bit of peanut butter to a slice of banana, and you've just created a doggy gourmet treat in your dog's eyes. The banana provides your pet with amino acids, electrolytes, fiber, manganese, potassium, minerals, and vitamins B6 and C.

Spinach: My dog (Wallace Braveheart) adores spinach, and it can be served in various ways that will provide your pet with the iron it contains.

Eggs: Eggs are a good source of protein for your dog and are also high in nutrients.

However, there are two potential problems with raw eggs: salmonella or E. coli food poisoning and the presence of avidin, a vitamin B inhibitor found in uncooked egg whites.

Blueberries: High in antioxidants, blueberries are an excellent superfood and a popular sweet treat among dogs. Blueberries can be added to your dog's meal, served on the side, or frozen for added crunch.

Pumpkin: We can purée pumpkin and freeze it for later use—it will keep in the freezer for months. Pumpkin is a good year-round food for your dog. Pumpkin is a great food for making your dog feel full and can help with diarrhea and constipation. You can also use canned pumpkin purée in this recipe.

Green beans: A great source of vitamin A, green beans also help your dog feel full without packing on the calories. If you do not have fresh green beans, you can use canned green beans, but choose a variety of low-sodium beans.

Types of Homemade Dog Food Diets

You will find not only traditional meals and foods in this book but also recipes that work for several special diets: paleo, raw, and grain-free. Below are some details about the dietary options:

Raw R: The raw canine diet is the most contentious. The raw diet is said to help dogs have cleaner teeth, better skin, and coats, but it is also thought to be a risk for spreading bacteria to both dogs and humans, especially when a dog has just finished eating a raw diet and then licks a toddler or senior citizen who later picks up a toy that the dog's saliva has all over. Some dog owners believe that feeding raw bones to their dogs is dangerous.

Paleo P: The Paleo diet mimics the hunter-gatherer diet, which more people are adopting for themselves. When dog owners change their diets, they may also consider their dog's diets and wonder what is the best diet for them.

Many dog owners believe a canine version of the Paleo diet, also known as an Ancestral Diet, is the best dog diet. It is a diet that is higher in protein and fat from meat and lower in carbohydrates than conventional diets.

Grain-free GF: Because more pet owners are concerned about the high levels of grains in traditional dog kibble, grain-free food is one of the fastest-growing segments of the commercial pet food industry. Dogs can eat grain, but they have a more difficult time digesting grains than humans, partly due to a lack of enzymes in their saliva to begin the digestion process. Some dogs are allergic to grains and may also be allergic to chicken, beef, and other meats.

The BARF Diet is another option. This one is based on the idea that dogs are omnivores and is based on an "ancestral" diet. It makes use of "biologically appropriate" foods such as meat, bones, organs, fruits, vegetables, and unprocessed supplements.

A third option is the Prey Model Raw (PMR) Diet. It is an animal-only diet that focuses on what dogs would eat in the wild. The ingredients are heavy on meat, bones, organs, and feathers, with no fruits or vegetables.

The DIY Homemade Dog Food Diet is the final option. This is essentially a whatever-works diet with no specific rules other than what works for your pet and provides them with the necessary nutrition. There is no specific food inclusion or exclusion. Unlike raw food models, these diets can include both cooked and uncooked foods and appropriate supplements.

This last option is often the most preferred of those in the pet industry. This is because it allows the pet owner to design recipes and meals that are completely nutritional and don't place any unreasonable rules or restrictions that may hinder a pet owner from creating a diet. This brings up the question of whether creating homemade food for your dog is right for you.

Transitioning From Store-Bought Food to Homemade

It is always easier for your dog's system to transition its diet gradually. If your dog is used to one type of kibble and you want to transition to homemade, start slowly. Begin the process with half a bag of kibble and gradually add the new homemade ingredients to the kibble. Begin with 30% new ingredients and 70% kibble, and adjust the ratio every few days until you reach 100% homemade. If your dog is used to a specific protein, such as chicken, start with the chicken recipes in this book. It's a good idea to keep this practice going when rotating recipes for variety.

When switching from one protein to another, use the same vegetables or fruits they've been eating for the past few days. The dog will then only be adapting to the protein change, while the rest of the recipe will be easier for its system to digest. You can experiment with the rest of the ingredients when they've adapted to the protein. If you think of homemade feeding as a long list of rotating ingredients, you can make gradual changes that keep your dog's system happy. If your dog was a wild animal, it would follow a similar pattern. They may eat the same vegetables in their habitat while hunting various types of protein at will.

Once you get the hang of this, the most efficient way to cook for your dog is by picking a couple of recipes, preparing a batch large enough to supply a week's worth of food, vacuum-sealing individual serving portions, and freezing them. To thaw, transfer the portions from the freezer to the refrigerator, one or two meals at a time, and allow the meals to thaw for about 24 hours.

CHAPTER 1
BENEFITS OF HOMEMADE FOOD FOR DOGS

Benefits of Homemade Dog Food

A variety of health problems, such as kidney, liver, and heart disease, can be managed with proper homemade dog food and veterinary care. A variety of ingredients can help with the conditions listed above. Homemade dog food can also benefit dogs of all ages, including puppies, adults, and seniors. Whatever your pet's level of health and wellness, homemade dog food can provide an enticing meal that benefits their body. Let's take a closer look at all of the advantages of feeding a homemade dog food diet.

Food Quality Control

Pet food recalls are becoming more common, which may cause you to be concerned about the quality and safety of your dog's food. Making your pet food diet allows you to control what goes into your pet's diet more than a commercial dog food diet does. Rather than simply choosing between meat and by-products, consider the cut of meat, where it comes from, and the overall quality of the meat.

Getting Rid of Filler Ingredients

Many commercial pet foods will use cheap filler ingredients to bulk up their foods. These filler materials frequently lack nutritional value. This enables businesses to produce large quantities of food at a lower cost. However, these ingredients frequently pass through a pet's system, resulting in more waste. Furthermore, filler ingredients are frequently the source of allergies. You can increase the nutritional value of your pet's food by eliminating fillers and potential food allergies when you make your homemade dog food.

Enhanced Variety

You'll probably end up feeding the same kibble for at least a month if you feed a commercial dog food diet. This can become tedious for your pet and reduce its nutritional value. With a homemade dog food recipe, you can change the ingredients regularly to provide your pet with a broader range of nutrients. The more diverse the nutrient sources in your pet's diet, the healthier they will be overall.

Nutritional Enhancement

While ingredient labels can be helpful, many commercial dog food labels are very cryptic when it comes to specifics. This means you're feeding your pet unknown and, in some cases, artificial ingredients. You can use whole foods and healthy ingredients when feeding a homemade pet food diet. You will also be able to avoid feeding questionable ingredients such as by-products.

Food That Is Not Preserved

Even the highest quality pet foods on the market contain artificial preservatives and added salts to keep the food fresh from the manufacturing plant to your home. These preservatives will not be present in homemade dog food because everything is made fresh. Preservatives frequently aggravate pre-existing health conditions, such as heart disease, leading to overall poor health. It is healthier to eat less preservatives and more fresh food, just as it is with humans.

Reduced Waste

You can use more dog-friendly leftovers from your human meals if you make your dog food. This lowers your household's food costs as well as food waste. You can even plan your family's meals ahead of time to save money and time on pet food preparation. Bulk protein sources, fruits, and vegetables will be available.

A Potentially Less Expensive Alternative

Certain pet foods, such as prescription diets or those with a distinct nutritional composition, frequently have higher manufacturing costs. This means that the cost is passed on to the pet owner, and these foods can be costly. Depending on the commercial diet you are feeding your pet, you may discover that making your pet food is less expensive. If you are simply feeding a generic diet, however, making a homemade diet may be more expensive. You must think about and break down the individual monthly costs.

Remove Allergens

If your pet has a sensitive stomach or another type of allergy, getting a diet free of allergens may not be enough. Dog food can be easily exposed to allergens during the manufacturing process or contain different allergens, such as chicken and chicken fat. When you make homemade pet food, you can control the exact ingredients and how they are prepared, allowing you to eliminate all allergens. You can consult a veterinarian or a nutritionist to find healthy alternatives.

While these are some of the many benefits you can get from a homemade dog food diet, this isn't to say they aren't without disadvantages. Let's also consider what are some of the downsides to making your pet food diet.

Cons of Homemade Dog Food

Of course, we're going to discuss the many advantages, but before I get started on all that, let's look at some of the drawbacks that cause people to shy away. (There is always an easier, more efficient way - we'll discuss that too.)

It's Time Consuming

Making homemade dog food will take some time. It truly depends on the quantity of food, the method, and the recipe. I mean, if you compare the time it takes to get a scoop of food out of store-bought food to the time it takes to make a batch of food, it will be much less time.

When you make homemade dog food, you also make a time commitment. Rather than simply scooping food into a bowl, you'll need to follow a few steps: measure, cook, portion, and store. A homemade dog food diet requires a lot of preparation. However, you can save time by cooking in bulk and then freezing leftovers for later use to reduce overall diet preparation time.

Nutritional Requirements

Providing your dog with the proper nutritional balance is critical to its health and well-being. We may be able to consume some of the same foods, but that does not imply that we should. A dog requires certain vitamins, minerals, and other nutrients. You'll need to know what your furry friends require to prepare a proper and healthy balanced meal for them. (I'll follow up on this as well.)

Some Diets Are Nutritionally Deficient

When preparing a homemade diet for your pet, just as you would for human food, it is critical to have the proper supplements and vitamins on hand to provide optimal nutrition. Many of the pet food recipes available online are not focused on specific dietary needs and do not include the necessary supplements and vitamins. This can result in a variety of health issues, including weight loss and decreased energy. To ensure that your homemade pet food is nutritionally sound, ensure that the recipes are created or overseen by a veterinarian or nutritionist.

Be Wary of Dangerous Ingredients

Most pet owners are aware of the dangers of certain human foods, such as chocolate, onions, raisins, grapes, and so on. However, not all recipes are created by people who are aware of potentially hazardous human ingredients. The best way to avoid using potentially dangerous ingredients in your pet food is to only use recipes approved by a veterinarian or nutritionist. You can also become acquainted with the entire list of human foods that are not suitable for dogs to consume.

Calories Too Many or Too Few

When feeding a commercial diet, simply read the back of the bag to determine how much to feed per day. You won't have access to this concise nutritional information when making a homemade recipe. Without this nutritional information, you may end up overfeeding or underfeeding your pet on a homemade diet. You must either prepare a recipe that includes the necessary nutritional information or calculate this information yourself.

Cost

If you know how to shop, you can shop anywhere. Making homemade dog food, or any type of pet food, can be costly in either case. To be honest, healthy eating for humans can be prohibitively expensive and should not be. Doctor and veterinarian bills appear to be far more expensive in the long run. Not to mention the emotional toll of losing your pet.

One of the most significant disadvantages of a homemade pet food diet is the cost. Commercial dog food can be inexpensive, whereas a homemade diet will require more expensive ingredients. However, you may still be able to find high-quality homemade dog food diets on a tight budget.

Inconvenient

When traveling, there are plenty of options for humans to eat. However, if you travel frequently, then having homemade dog food isn't that convenient. A lot of boarding facilities can't accommodate feeding a homemade dog food diet, and traveling with homemade dog food is even more difficult. When traveling, most people revert to commercial dog foods for convenience.

CHAPTER 2
COMMON MISTAKES AND FOODS TO AVOID

Common Mistakes with Homemade Dog Food

When it comes to the pet industry, simply hearing something from an advertisement or another pet owner does not always make it true. Pet owners believe in numerous myths about everything from grooming to food. When it comes to your pet's food, incorrect information can have disastrous consequences. Let's take a look at some of the most common myths about homemade dog food, recipes, and the cooking process to ensure you have the right information before you get started.

Being Under the Impression That Multivitamins Provide a Well-Balanced Meal

It is believed that incorporating a multivitamin into a cooked homemade diet will compensate for any nutritional deficiencies. This is not entirely correct. Depending on the recipe, some supplements must be included while others must be avoided. A single multivitamin will not solve the problem because they are not designed to be used in conjunction with a homemade diet. While some vitamins and minerals are required to improve the nutritional structure of a homemade diet, most multivitamins are intended to supplement a commercial dog food diet that is already nutritionally balanced. This means that your pet's diet will still be deficient in essential vitamins and minerals. The bioavailability of supplements must also be considered.

Choosing Ingredients Rather Than Supplements

A pet owner might be told to supplement a meal with cottage cheese or yogurt if their pet is deficient in calcium to supplement the diet. However, calculating the pet's specific needs and how much you are adding through the foods is difficult. The nutrients that a dog will require through supplementation are frequently required in higher concentrations than simple food ingredients can provide. This means you won't be able to include enough nutrients without increasing the number of calories. Supplements are sometimes more important than ingredients, but not in all.

Vegetables Are Preferable

The misconception frequently misleads those who focus on a homemade diet that adding fruits and vegetables to a diet is important because they provide additional vitamins and nutritional variety. Dogs, on the other hand, are not omnivorous like other animals. This means they thrive on a diet high in animal protein and their digestive system cannot handle large amounts of vegetables. Adding a lot of vegetables to your pet's diet will not improve their health and may even cause digestive problems. Some fruits and vegetables are beneficial, but don't overdo it.

A Well-Balanced Human Meal Is the Same As a Well-Balanced Dog Meal

Humans are omnivores who eat protein, carbohydrates, and fats. All of these macronutrients are focused on meeting a human's daily needs with a well-balanced meal. On the other hand, dogs are carnivorous scavengers who eat mostly animal protein and a small amount of grain, fruits, and vegetables. The macronutrient ratio required by dogs differs from that required by humans.

Multiple Diets Help to Achieve Balance

Because many recipes contain the same deficiencies, the approach of using multiple diets to create a balanced diet for your dog is false.

Impact of Dietary Changes

When you choose to make homemade food for your dog, you should always do it under the guidance of someone experienced. You'll need to consider your dog's eating history, weight, and overall health when finding the right recipe for their diet. You want to ensure you are feeding a diet with the right impact, and you'll want to continue monitoring your pet's health while transitioning to a homemade diet. So now, let's look at what you need to include in a balanced homemade diet by considering the nutritional guidelines.

What Foods Should Your Dog Never Eat?

Some dogs, like humans, have food allergies that cause digestive issues ranging from farts to diarrhea.

As a dog owner, you've probably seen this list before, but it's always useful to have it on hand as a reminder, especially if you're making dog food from scratch. The following are the most dangerous foods:

Chocolate

It is not advisable to feed chocolate to pets. Chocolate contains theobromine, a chemical related to caffeine.

Because theobromine is not quickly digested, the dog is especially sensitive to even a small dose. Theobromine has a half-life of 6 hours in humans but 17.5 hours in dogs.

Garlic and Onions

Onions contain n-propyl disulfide, which may harm the lipid membranes of red blood cells if consumed. This membrane damage causes hemoglobin to become permanently denatured, forming Heinz bodies in red blood cells. The result is Heinz's anemia, a condition in which red blood cells are damaged. Heinz body anemia is a condition that affects dogs.

While garlic may be beneficial to dogs in small doses, excessive amounts can be harmful.

Garlic is related to onions, which are harmful to dogs because they destroy their red blood cell levels, resulting in anemia.

Weakness, vomiting, and breathing difficulties are all possible symptoms.

Raisins and Grapes

Some dogs develop clinical signs of acute renal failure within 48 hours of consuming what appears to be a small amount of raisins or grapes.

Sugary Foods and Drinks

Avoid giving your dog anything high in processed sugars when it comes to cookies. She will experience the same side effects that humans do when they consume too much sugar: weight gain, tooth decay, and possibly diabetes.

Caffeine

It contains a stimulant that is harmful to dogs. While you may enjoy a cup of coffee in the morning, your dog should stick to the tried-and-true water.

Salt

Too much salt can cause dehydration and sodium ion poisoning. While a small amount of salt is beneficial, keep track of how much your dog consumes to keep the amount to a minimum.

Cherries

Cherries are poisonous because their pits, leaves, and stems contain cyanide. Every now and then, a couple of cherries that have been seeded and de-stemmed are fine. Not too many and not too frequently. There are no seeds, stems, or leaves.

Nightshade

Any plant that is in the Nightshade family, such as tomatoes or eggplant. Potatoes are a part of the Nightshade family, too, but as long as they are cooked, they're safe for your dog to eat.

Random Mushrooms

Dogs can typically eat mushrooms that are safe for human consumption. However, out in the wild, they should not eat any random mushroom that you can't positively identify as safe.

Rhubarb Leaves

Rhubarb leaves are toxic. The stems are non-toxic and can be beneficial for constipated dogs.

Macadamia Nuts

In small amounts, macadamia nuts can be toxic. The side effects are usually mild and can be managed at home, but this is not always the case. If your dog consumes any of these nuts, look for symptoms such as weakness in the back legs, diarrhea, and vomiting. You should contact your veterinarian.

The Ice Cream

I'm not sure who would want to include ice cream in their homemade dog food recipe, but someone may do. DO NOT DO IT IF YOU ARE THAT PERSON. Milk can be difficult for dogs to digest. This sweet treat also contains a lot of sugar, so either way, it's not going to be good.

Nutmeg

Nutmeg is toxic to dogs. It is unquestionably a NO. Too much nutmeg can also be toxic to humans. Myristicin, which is found in nutmeg, is a natural insecticide.

By removing these foods, your dog will immediately become happier and healthier. And, with a well-balanced diet and regular exercise, your pet will undoubtedly appreciate you. Even if she is disappointed that she was unable to consume a slice of your macadamia nut cookie.

Blue Cheese

Like other dairy products, cheese is difficult for dogs to digest, and higher-fat varieties present additional difficulties. Blue cheese is particularly dangerous to dogs because it contains stilton and Roquefort cheese. Some dogs are extremely sensitive to roquefortine C, which is found in a variety of blue cheeses.

When dogs consume roquefortine C, they may vomit or have diarrhea. Dogs suffering from large overdoses may also experience tremors, seizures, and fever.

Corn on the Cob

The problem isn't the corn in this case; it's the cob. If you want to feed your dog corn, give it to him whole. The cob itself is brittle and difficult to digest for dogs.

Effects: The cob is a choking hazard and may cause gastrointestinal blockages. Blockages necessitate immediate surgery to correct the problem; otherwise, death may result.

Food That Has Mold On It

You usually throw moldy foods away; just ensure they're in a garbage can that your dog can't get into. Moldy foods, such as bread and dairy products, contain fungal neurotoxins that are harmful to your dog if she consumes them.

Side effects of a dog eating moldy foods include vomiting, diarrhea, tremors, seizures, and fever. These symptoms can appear between 24 and 48 hours and can be fatal if not treated.

Plum pits, like cherry pits, are a source of concern with this fruit. Plum pits contain cyanide as well, and a dog who eats some plum pits is destined for medical problems.

Ingestion of plum pits, like cherry pits, can cause bowel blockages, difficulty breathing, and death in dogs.

Xylitol (Artificial Sweeteners) (Artificial Sweeteners)

Xylitol, a common additive, is an artificial sweetener that is commonly found in sugar-free foods. It is also found in cough syrups, chewable and gummy vitamins, nasal sprays, laxatives, and human prescription medications, among other things, so make sure your dog does not have access to any of these items if they are in your home.

Because of its effect on insulin regulation in the body, xylitol can cause low blood sugar (hypoglycemia) and liver failure in dogs. Fatigue, loss of coordination, and vomiting are symptoms of xylitol poisoning.

Apples, while apple fruit is safe in small amounts, apple seeds are not because they contain cyanide. Apple cores are also a serious choking hazard. Only give your dog sliced, unseeded apples.

Apricots, like apples, are safe for dogs to eat; however, the seeds are poisonous. Apricot seeds contain cyanide, and the pit is large enough to cause a choking hazard or blockage if swallowed whole.

Keep this list of foods that your dog should never eat nearby. If you see your dog eat one of these items or suspect she has, contact your veterinarian immediately or your local or national poison control center. Use this opportunity to educate yourself on what foods to keep away from your dog and to motivate yourself to clean your kitchen so that no harmful foods are within reach of your puppy's mouth.

Some foods are not necessarily harmful to dogs but should be fed to them with extreme caution. Not all dogs react the same way to the same food; just as humans can be allergic to certain foods, so can dogs. Trial and error are fine, but you don't want to mess with your dog's health and well-being. Here are some foods to avoid before introducing them into your dog's diet.

CHAPTER 3
NUTRITIONAL GUIDELINES

The first thing to consider is what constitutes a complete and balanced diet for a dog, which includes proteins, fats, carbohydrates, vitamins, and minerals. Water is another essential component of a well-balanced diet, and it is required daily. These are very simple ways to break down the basic components of a well-balanced diet, but there is a lot more to consider. You must understand how each nutrient is used in the body, the processes involved, and how much of each nutrient is required to provide adequate health for your dog at all life stages.

Your canine companion requires a balanced diet for optimal health and welfare, just as we humans do. With the right nutrition, your dog can grow and develop to its full potential, giving him the energy and excitement to engage in both physical and mental activities.

Your dog's dietary habits may affect both his behavior and health. There is a direct link between better behavior and a biologically appropriate, well-balanced diet. A balanced diet of high-quality foods can help your dog feel less stressed and more at ease by lowering his stress levels. Giving your dog the nutrition he needs will make him less likely to develop bad habits. The quality of the source of the essential nutrients required by a dog is also important. A well-balanced, nutritious canine diet should only contain premium ingredients; it should not contain extraneous ingredients such as food coloring, unidentified animal byproducts, or chemical preservatives. The majority of animal nutritionists agree with this.

Dogs' energy requirements may vary depending on a variety of factors. It is critical to meet your dog's specific energy needs to support its daily lifestyle. Some of the contributing factors are growth, reproduction (unaltered vs. altered), adult age groups (young, middle, and older), activity level, breed, and medical and behavioral issues.

The majority of the energy in the diet comes from fats and proteins, with Carbs coming in second. A diet's caloric content determines the quality of the food and the recommended daily calorie intake. The food should meet your dog's daily energy requirements. All nutrients must be balanced for optimal absorption by the body and appropriate utilization by each biological system. Your dog's digestive system will be unable to physically ingest enough of the diet if it lacks sufficient energy, and it will be unable to obtain the nutrients they require.

For example, dogs on an energy-rich diet will consume less food overall. In this case, it is critical to ensure that the percentage of other vital nutrients consumed is sufficient to compensate for the lower volume consumed. A feeding study is the only way to determine whether a meal has enough energy to ensure sufficient ingredients to maintain a healthy everyday life.

Proteins

Proteins are required to form and maintain cartilage, tendons, and ligaments. Furthermore, protein in dog food aids in the production of blood, muscle, skin, hair, and nails. When protein is broken down, amino acids are produced, which are vital nutrients for dogs. Amino acids are required by dogs' bodies to produce energy and maintain life. Dogs require ten essential amino acids to live a healthy life. Because the body is unable to produce these nutrients, they must be obtained through diet.

Protein is an important part of a dog's diet because it contains amino acids that are necessary for growth. In terms of food quality, protein from animal sources is superior to protein from vegetable sources. Meat and egg proteins have a complete amino acid profile, whereas vegetable proteins lack some. Vegetables can still provide significant amounts of protein for your dog, but they must be combined with other types of protein.

Protein is found in every body cell, making it an essential component of meals. Your dog and you both require it to maintain your body's structure. Protein is also needed in greater quantities due to physical activity and the need for growing pups. The higher the protein quality, the less it is required by the dog. The more exercise a dog gets, the higher their protein requirement. In addition, in unusual circumstances, such as illness or recuperation, our dog's protein demand increases. The most important factors influencing a dog's protein requirement are pregnancy and nursing.

Animal protein sources contain the highest concentrations of essential amino acids. Plant-based proteins are typically less digestible in dogs because they cannot digest plant fiber as efficiently as other types of fiber. In theory, dogs can survive on a protein-only plant-based diet, but this diet may necessitate a variety of protein sources to achieve a daily minimum that can be safely absorbed.

Carbohydrates

One of the main functions of carbohydrates in a dog's diet is to provide energy. Because they supply dietary fiber and energy in the form of glucose, carbohydrates are essential to a dog's daily diet. The body needs glucose; if it cannot get it from carbohydrates, it will divert amino acids from other bodily functions.

Furthermore, carbohydrates generate heat within the body, serve as the foundation for additional nutrition, and have the potential to become fat (some carbohydrates). Dogs and growing animals should be fed a diet containing at least 20% carbohydrates.

Fiber, a type of carbohydrate, is essential for a dog's digestive system to function properly. It helps to keep the colon healthy by working with the bacteria in the gut. The fiber measurement is provided as crude fiber (the insoluble portions). Total dietary fiber is made up of both soluble and insoluble fibers.

Carbohydrates are your dog's primary source of energy. Carbohydrates feed cells with glucose and can be converted into glycogen, which is stored in the muscles and liver. Carbohydrates are not required for dogs to consume, but they provide more energy than other sources of energy.

Carbohydrates can be obtained from vegetables. Dogs can convert vegetables into glucose for energy, but it requires more effort than obtaining the same amount of energy from a meat-based diet.

Carbohydrates should be limited if your dog is overweight. It's a simple way to help your dog lose weight.

A lack of fatty acids may aggravate some dermatological diseases, slow wound healing, and result in dull, lifeless hair. High-fat diets necessitate more vitamin E supplementation because it is involved in antioxidant protection. To absorb fat-soluble vitamins, 1% to 2% of the food must contain fat.

Essential fatty acids are found in a variety of foods and are beneficial to a dog's health. Linoleic acid is the precursor to arachidonic acid, an essential omega-6 fatty acid (LA).

Omega-3 fatty acids help reduce inflammation caused by conditions such as arthritis, some cancers, burns, dermatitis, inflammatory bowel disease, and kidney disease. Omega-3 fatty acids play an important role in the health and functionality of cartilage. Marine fish, flaxseed, and canola oils contain omega-3 fatty acids.

Soluble Fiber

Soluble fiber's ability to retain water softens dog feces in general. Soluble fiber is commonly found in fruits and gums (a group of viscous, sticky polysaccharides found in seeds and plants). A variety of soluble fibers can also be fermented. A dog's healthy gut bacteria can use fermentable fibers as a source of energy. They also produce short-chain fatty acids, which intestinal cells can use as an energy source (called prebiotics).

Sugar is found in both honey and fruits. Starch (a polysaccharide) can be obtained in adequate amounts by dogs from foods such as corn, wheat, rice, barley, oats, and potatoes.

Fats

Fats are solid lipids composed primarily of triglycerides at room temperature. Dietary fat is pet food's most concentrated energy source (2.25 times the number of calories compared to proteins or carbohydrates). The body uses fat for various purposes, including energy production and the absorption of fat-soluble vitamins. One of the most important tasks is to provide the necessary fatty acids (EFAs). EFAs help dogs maintain healthy skin and coat quality while also reducing cellular inflammation. The polyunsaturated fatty acids omega-3 and omega-6 are both important.

Fat plays a significant role in your dog's diet. The best fat comes from animal sources because their bodies can process it more easily than plant-based fats. Fat indeed has 9 calories per gram, but your dog needs it for energy and to absorb vitamins such as A, D, and E.

Water Requirements

Water is considered one of the most important nutrients because it performs a variety of functions, including the following:

- Body temperature control
- Fat, protein, and carbohydrate breakdown
- Providing body structure and shape
- Keeping the shape of your eyes
- Lubrication of joints
- Nervous system defense

Dogs get additional water through their diet in addition to drinking water. A normal, healthy, and altered dog's daily water requirement is 2.5 times the dry matter they eat. Another way to look at it is that a dog should drink enough water each day to equal the amount of energy or food that they consume. This can be affected by a variety of factors that affect the body, including age, gender, size, stress, and others. It is also affected by the amount of dry matter consumed through diet.

In general, dogs who are fed a moist diet will drink less water during the day because their food contains more moisture. Dogs should always have constant access to clean and fresh water. It is also critical to monitor your dog's daily intake and notify your veterinarian if there is a decrease or increase.

Before we get further into the homemade dog food diet, let's take a moment to consider commercial dog foods and how to determine quality.

Vitamins

A dog's body uses vitamins for various purposes, including DNA synthesis, bone formation, blood coagulation, normal eye function, and neurologic function.

To be classified as a vitamin, a nutrient must possess the following five characteristics:

- It must be an organic substance that is not a protein, carbohydrate, or fat.
- It is a crucial part of the diet.
- Normal function necessitates only trace amounts.
- Absence causes a deficit or reduces normal functioning.
- It cannot be produced in sufficient quantities by the body to support normal function.

Overdosing on vitamins and other nutrients can result in toxicity and other complications. Because multiple vitamins are occasionally required to complete a reaction, vitamin deficiencies have the potential to cascade. Because natural food items vary, it's critical to keep an eye on the sources of vitamins in a dog's diet to avoid deficiencies and overdoses (liver, lungs). Taking a vitamin and mineral supplement may be preferable to ensure adequate levels.

Dogs require a variety of vitamins in their diet. They are classified into two categories: fat-soluble and water-soluble.

Bile salts and fat are required to absorb fat-soluble vitamins in a dog's intestines. The four fat-soluble vitamins are A, D, E, and K. Because of how the body stores and uses fat-soluble vitamins; they are the most vulnerable to depletion and/or toxicity.

Vitamin A

Vitamin A, also known as retinol, is required for healthy skin, normal growth, reproduction, and vision. A vitamin A deficiency can cause skin problems and night blindness. Toxicity can result from over-supplementation, which can cause bleeding and irregular bone growth and formation. Fish oil is one of the most concentrated natural sources of vitamin A. Products derived from milk, eggs, and liver.

Because vitamin A is not stable on its own, a protective coating is often required to ensure absorption. Anorexia, stunted growth, a lifeless coat of hair, and frailty can all result from deficiencies. Toxins can cause growth retardation, anorexia, and bone fractures.

Vitamin D

Because dogs cannot produce vitamin D, also known as cholecalciferol (D3) and ergocalciferol (D2), it is essential for their health. Vitamin D aids in the absorption of calcium and phosphorus in the intestine and the retention of calcium and phosphorus in the bone. It si well-known that marine seafood and fish oil provide the highest natural sources, but excessive consumption can lead to an overdose. Additional sources include freshwater fish, eggs, meat, liver, and the majority of dairy products. Vitamin D3 and vitamin D2 supplements are the two primary synthetic sources.

Deficiencies can cause osteoporosis, rickets, swollen joints, and other bone problems. Toxic symptoms include hypercalcemia, decreased appetite or anorexia, and lameness.

Vitamin E

It works as an antioxidant in the body. In dogs, deficiency can cause decreased appetite or anorexia, skin, immunological issues, and neurological disorders. It is the least harmful fat-soluble vitamin. Although toxicity is rare, it can have an impact on blood clotting times and bone mineralization. Plants are the only ones that produce vitamin E.

Menadione

A type of vitamin K, helps with blood clotting and bone growth.

There is no recommended vitamin K dosage for dogs, though the AAFCO recommends 1.64 mg/kg for both adults and puppies.

A lack of vitamin K can cause bleeding and slow clotting times. They can be caused by underlying medical conditions that impair the gut's ability to absorb vitamin K. (such as inflammatory bowel disease). Anemia and jaundice have been linked to specific forms of vitamin K. If your veterinarian recommends supplements, inquire about the best sources of vitamin K for your pet. Excellent sources of vitamin K include alfalfa meal, oilseed meal, liver, and fish meal.

Omega-6

Is essential for coat care, resulting in rich, lustrous fur for your dog. Adding sunflower or safflower oil (about 1 tsp for a small dog or 1 tbsp for a large dog) to your dog's diet can help keep his coat shiny.

Omega-3 fatty acids benefit your dog's skin and can be found in flaxseed oil or fish oil (including sardines, one of our dogs' favorites).

Minerals

Minerals are the primary structural components of organs and tissues, as well as body fluids, electrolytes, and muscle contractions. Minerals are also involved in the enzyme and hormone systems and can be subdivided into two categories: macrominerals and trace minerals. Both are required by dogs in varying amounts. Without a completely balanced mineral profile in a dog's body, many biological systems will begin to fail, causing serious medical problems and, in some cases, death.

These minerals must be present in concentrations greater than 100mg/Mcal. The following are examples of macrominerals:

Calcium (Ca)

Is a mineral essential for teeth and bones' health and appearance. It is also required for cell communication, blood clotting, muscle function, and nerve transmission. The bones and teeth contain nearly 99% of all calcium in a dog. An imbalance in the phosphorus-calcium levels can result from too much or too little calcium. This can result in bone reabsorption, stunted growth, anorexia, limping, lameness, bone fracturing, loose teeth, and convulsions. Low calcium levels have been linked to kidney dysfunction, pancreatitis, and eclampsia. Calcium supplementation may be required, but only under the supervision of a veterinarian due to the increased risk of mineral imbalance. Calcium supplementation in excess can cause limb lameness and joint swelling. It can also result in medical conditions such as secondary hyperparathyroidism.

Phosphorus (P)

Is a mineral that is essential for many tissues and bodily functions. It is the second most abundant structural component in bones, teeth, RNA, and DNA. It aids in cell growth, energy utilization, and the formation of amino acids and proteins. The AAFCO recommendation for growing puppies is 0.8%, and for adults, maintenance is 0.5%.

Phosphorus

Is primarily found in animal-based ingredients in a dog's diet. As phytic acid, plant-based ingredients have a low phosphorus content. Phosphorus levels are highest in meat tissues, which include poultry, lamb, fish, and beef. Phosphorus levels are highest in eggs, milk, oilseeds, protein supplements, and grains.

Pica, decreased growth, a poor hair coat, and bone fractures can all result from a lack of phosphorus. Too much phosphorus in the diet can cause bone loss, urinary stones, weight loss, and calcification of tissues and organs.

Magnesium (Mg)

Magnesium is involved in bone formation, carbohydrate and fat metabolism, and neuromuscular activity. For growing puppies, AAFCO recommends 0.04% DM and 0.08% DM for adult maintenance. Magnesium is best found in bone products such as bone meal or lamb meal, oilseeds, flaxseed, soybean meal, unrefined grains, and fibers.

Magnesium deficiency can cause stunted growth, muscle contraction, and mobility problems, as well as decreased eating or anorexia. Excess magnesium can cause stone formation and paralysis. The kidneys are in charge of magnesium regulation. Certain drugs and medical conditions can also cause a magnesium imbalance.

Potassium (K)

Is the most abundant mineral found within cells. It aids in many bodily functions, including acid-base balance and osmotic balance. It also helps in nerve impulse transmission and muscle contraction. Potassium is not stored in the body and must be obtained through diet. For all life stages, the AAFCO recommends 0.6% DM. Among sources of potassium, we can find soybean meal, unrefined grains, fiber sources, and yeast. A lack of potassium can cause anorexia, lethargy, and difficulty walking. Too much potassium is uncommon, but it can cause heart and muscle problems.

Chloride and Sodium (Na) (Cl)

These minerals help to maintain osmotic pressure, acid-base balance, and what enters and exits the cells in the body. Sodium also aids in the absorption of calcium and water-soluble vitamins. A lack of one or both of these minerals can result in anorexia, weakness, fatigue, and hair loss. Too much of either is uncommon unless there is a lack of good, clean water; however, if it does occur, it can cause constipation, seizures, and, in rare cases, death.

Mineral Traces

These, also known as microminerals, are required in amounts less than 100mg/Mcal.

Iron (Fe) is a mineral that is essential for oxygen transport throughout the body. Anemia, a rough coat, lethargy, and stunted growth can all result from a lack of iron. For all life stages, AAFCO recommends 80mg/kg. Most meat ingredients contain iron, particularly organ meats such as liver, spleen, and lungs. It is also present in some Fiber: sources. Too much iron in the diet can lead to anorexia, weight loss, and liver problems.

Copper (Cu) (Cu)

Copper plays a significant role in the body by supporting the creation and activity of enzymes, promoting hemoglobin formation and oxygen transportation, contributing to cardiac function, aiding in bone and myelin formation, facilitating connective tissue development, and supporting immune function. The liver is the primary site of copper metabolism. For all life stages, AAFCO recommends at least 7.3mg/kg DM.

Most meats are high in copper, with organ meats from cattle having the highest concentration. The amount of copper available in food varies, making it a difficult mineral to supplement. A lack of copper can result in abnormal growth, hair color changes, bone problems, and neurological conditions. Some dog breeds are prone to liver toxicity as a result of excessive copper consumption. A high copper intake can cause hepatitis and an increase in liver enzymes.

Zinc (Zn)

Zinc participates in more than one hundred enzyme functions, such as protein synthesis, metabolism of carbohydrates, healing of skin and wounds, and functioning of the immune system. Zinc is not a toxic substance in and of itself, but too much of it can interact with other minerals and reduce their absorption. For all life stages, AAFCO recommends 120mg/kg DM. Meats and fiber-rich foods contain the most zinc.

Insufficient zinc levels may cause reduced desire to eat, inhibited development, balding, compromised immunity, and growth disorders. Some arctic dog breeds may suffer from zinc deficiency, which may necessitate supplementation even with adequate food intake.

Manganese (Mn)

Is a mineral that is involved in many body systems, including fat and carbohydrate metabolism, bone and cartilage development, and cell division. The AAFCO recommendation for all life stages is 5mg/kg DM. Manganese is present in Fiber: and fish meals. Too little manganese can cause bone deformities and poor growth.

Selenium (Se)

It is a mineral that helps the immune system function, protects cells from oxidative damage, and supports normal thyroid function. For all life stages, AAFCO recommends 0.11mg/kg. Selenium-rich foods include fish, eggs, and liver. Selenium deficiency is uncommon because Vitamin E can serve as a substitute in some functions.

A prolonged deficiency, on the other hand, can result in a decrease in eating and edema in the body. The overabundance of selenium has the potential to result in emesis, muscular contractions, loss of balance and feebleness, excessive salivation, reduced food intake or anorectic behavior, breathing difficulties, noxious breath scent, and mouth malodor, in addition to complications with nails.

Iodine (I)

It is a mineral that is essential for the proper functioning of the thyroid. One of the functions of the thyroid gland is to regulate body temperature and aid in growth, development, skin and hair repair, as well as neuromuscular function. For all life stages, AAFCO recommends 1.5mg/kg DM.

Iodine-rich foods include fish, eggs, and iodized salts. Calcium iodate, potassium iodide, and cuprous iodide are common supplements found in commercial foods. Goiter, enlarged thyroid glands, hair loss, lethargy, weakness, decreased eating or anorexia, and fever are all symptoms of too much or too little iodine.

Magnesium

Magnesium is thought to have stress-relieving properties. If the mineral is adequately supplied to the body, it can result in increased cortisol release, which means it affects the production of stress hormones. Magnesium relaxes and soothes the body by dampening nerve transmission.

Stress raises the demand for magnesium by increasing the mineral's consumption in cells and its excretion. Magnesium should be given to a dog who is constantly under stress.

Calcium

Calcium is an important component of your dog's diet. Calcium is essential for the development and maintenance of bones and teeth. Dogs must have access to calcium-rich food because they cannot produce or absorb it on their own.

Calcium should be added to a dog's diet if he or she is neutered, pregnant, lactating, ill, or growing. Calcium deficiency in your dog can cause urinary system malfunction and severe health problems later in life.

Calcium has some indirect effects too—for example, it can affect your dog's temperament.

You'll find a method for producing your own eggshell calcium in this book, which many pet owners prefer to bone meal because bones can store calcium. Since eggshells are composed of calcium carbonate, they contain great amounts of the mineral.

Allergies

Dogs can be affected by food allergies, which are among the most common allergies or hypersensitivities. Allergic pets have an immune system that goes into overdrive, creating antibodies for substances it would usually ignore. Antibodies are produced against a specific food component, which is typically a protein or complex carbohydrate. Food allergies typically appear after repeated exposure to a single brand, type, or form of food because an allergy requires the production of antibodies to develop.

Food allergies in dogs typically manifest as hives on the skin, paws, or ears, as well as stomach issues such as vomiting or diarrhea. There may be other changes that are not as obvious, like hyperactivity, weight loss, fatigue, and even hostility.

Proteins, particularly those derived from dairy, beef, chicken eggs, soy, or wheat gluten, are the main culprits behind the most frequent food allergies in dogs. Symptoms occur when a pet consumes food with these ingredients, causing an interaction between antibodies and antigens. However, almost any food ingredient has the potential to cause an allergic reaction. Proteins are the most common offenders, but other elements and additives may also be to blame.

There is no treatment for food allergies in dogs. The only available treatment is avoidance. Some dogs will require medication if their symptoms are severe, but the majority of canines can be successfully treated with a hypoallergenic diet.

When a dog develops an allergy to one food, he or she may develop allergies to other foods in the future. Furthermore, many dogs with food allergies also have other allergies, such as atopy (an allergy to inhalants or the environment) or a flea allergy. If you suspect your pet has a food allergy, consult with your veterinarian so that your pet can return to a healthier, more comfortable lifestyle.

How much Should My Dog Eat?

Obesity is a problem in the dog world, just as it is in humans. What's the reason? Most dog owners overfeed their pets. Feeding instructions on commercial food bags are just that: instructions. They are written for adult dogs who are not neutered; spayed and neutered dogs have lower metabolic rates and require slightly less food. Furthermore, many pet parents do not measure their dog's portions, instead simply filling the plate or (worse) "free feeding" with a bowl full of food that the dog is free to eat at any time of day.

Instead, measure out your dog's food for twice-daily feedings. (A recommended feeding schedule for puppies is three to four times daily). The general rule is that your dog should consume about 2.5% of his body weight per day. You'll adjust this up or down depending on your dog's activity level and whether you're trying to maintain, trim, or gain weight. That equates to about 2.5 pounds of food per day, or 1.25 pounds of food per meal, for a 100-pound dog.

Breed/Average Weight	Daily Serving
Chihuahua/6 pounds	.15 pound per day
Shetland Sheepdog/20 pounds	.5 pound per day
Dachshund/20-25 pounds	.5-.625 pound per day
Beagle/25 pounds	.625 pound per day
Poodle/45-70 pounds	1.125-1.75 pounds per day
Bulldog/50 pounds	1.25 pounds per day
Golden Retriever/60-80 pounds	1.5-2 pounds per day
Labrador Retriever/75 pounds	1.875 pounds per day
German Shepherd/75-95 pounds	1.875-2.25 pounds per day
Greyhound/80 pounds	2 pounds per day
Rottweiler/90-110 pounds	2.25-2.75 pounds per day
Great Dane/120 pounds	3 pounds per day

This is, of course, a very broad guide, one that varies with the food you're feeding, your dog's activity level, your dog's age, and any relevant medical conditions. (During cold weather, if your dog will be hiking outdoors with you, he will require additional food. If your dog is pregnant, she'll need more food.) This table provides a general baseline to work from as you see if your dog is still hungry after the meal or if your dog is gaining/losing weight.

You'll notice that the recipes in this book frequently produce far more than a dog could consume in a single sitting. Use this table to calculate how much food your dog requires per day, and then plan appropriate serving sizes for his meals and treats. Use the storage instructions provided to safely store and/or freeze any leftover prepared food.

Although indulgent dog guardians may fail to notice that their pooch is gaining weight, it is simple to ask your veterinarian if your dog is overweight. You can then keep track of your dog's weight by feeling his ribs regularly. He is usually not overweight if you can feel his ribs. Your dog's ribs should feel similar to the back of your hand. Examine your dog from above to see if his waist is visible. Tapering from behind his rib cage to his tail should be visible. You should also be able to see an upward "tummy tuck" in his abdomen from the side.

Making a Feeding Schedule

Whether you feed your dog a homemade diet, a commercial diet, or a combination of both, a feeding schedule is essential. Your goal is to ensure that your dogs receive adequate nutrition without becoming overweight. Overweight dogs, like overweight humans, are prone to a variety of health problems, including increased joint stress, lethargy, liver disease, and diabetes.

Although an adult dog can get enough nutrition from one large meal per day, splitting it up into two smaller meals served twice a day may reduce the risk of bloat, especially if your dog wolfs down his food. It also provides you with twice as many opportunities to bond with your dog through homemade food! Mealtime can also be used as a quick training exercise, with your dog sitting and politely waiting for your "okay" signal before diving in to enjoy the meal.

How Many Calories Does My Dog Require Daily?

Many factors, including your dog's size and metabolism, influence the type, amount, and frequency of calories they consume. Obesity can develop as a result of overfeeding your dog with excess energy. A variety of health problems can arise from this. As a result, your dog's health re-

quires that they consume the appropriate amount of food. Veterinarians have developed a formula to estimate your dog's calorie requirements.
(Body weight of your dog in kilograms x 30) + 70 = RER * * RER: Resting Energy Requirement
The calculated value represents the calorie requirement per day in the absence of any activity.

The RER is multiplied by a factor that accounts for your dog's living situation to calculate the actual calorie requirement:

- Adult neutered dog who is normally active: 1.6 x RER
- Adult, normally active dog who has not been neutered: 1.8 x RER
- Your dog performs light labor: 2 x RER
- Your dog works moderately: 3 x RER
- Your dog does heavy lifting: 4-8 x RER
- If your dog is pregnant (42 days), multiply by 1.8.
- Three times RER if your dog is pregnant (three weeks before the birth).
- Your puppy is suckling: 4-8 x RER (depending on how many puppies need to be looked after) (depending on how many puppies need to be looked after)
- If your puppy is less than four months old: 3 x RER
- Your dog is over four months old but not yet an adult: 2 x RER
- Your dog should shed some pounds: 1 x RER

As an example, consider my dog Max, a five-year-old mixed breed weighing 13 kilograms and being neutered.

13 kg multiplied by 30 + 70 = 460 calories (RER)

460 times 1.6 RER = 736 calories per day

According to this calculation, Max should be consuming 736 calories per day. To meet his demands, we must first know how many calories are in the daily diet.

CHAPTER 4
SUPPLEMENTS TO BE USED TO OPTIMIZE DIET

When you feed your pet a completely balanced and formulated diet, they will receive all the daily vitamins they require. Diets with an AAFCO statement are complete and balanced, containing all of the required vitamins. When selecting supplements for your homemade dog food diet, look for products with the National Animal Supplement Council's quality seal (NASC). This ensures that the products you receive have adequate bioavailability and safety. If your pet suffers from a medical condition, ensure that you supplement their food under the supervision of a veterinarian or nutritionist.

Water-soluble vitamin supplements are easily absorbed and utilized by a dog's body. Deficits are common because they are quickly depleted, and the body has no place to store them.

The following are the necessary water-soluble vitamin supplements for dogs:

Thiamin B1 (B1)

Thiamin (B1) supports the nervous system and participates in numerous enzymatic reactions throughout the body. Sources of thiamin-rich foods include whole grains, yeast, and liver. Animal meat and tissue are also good sources. Thiamin deficiency is uncommon because modern dog food contains adequate amounts of vitamins. A deficit can cause anemia or decreased appetite, weight loss, weakened muscles, seizures, ataxia, and enlarged hearts, to name a few heart and neurological system issues. Overdose can cause low blood pressure and heart and lung problems.

Riboflavin B2 (B2)

Riboflavin (B2) is required for several processes in the body of a dog.

Although they are uncommon, deficiencies can result in developmental delays, weight loss, neurological issues, skin, heart, and eye problems. Overdoses are rare and rarely harmful.

Pyridoxine B6 (B6)

Pyridoxine, a B6 vitamin, is required for amino acid metabolism as well as other biological functions. It also aids in the production of neurotransmitters. Meats, whole grains, vegetables, and nuts are the foods highest in vitamin B6.

Anorexia (loss of appetite), weight loss, growth restriction, anemia, convulsions, weakness, and kidney problems are all symptoms of deficiencies. Even if they appear to be rare, toxins can cause ataxia, signs of weakness, and falling over.

Niacin B3 (B3)

Niacin is involved in a variety of physiological and enzymatic processes in the diet of dogs (B3). Yeast, animal or fish byproducts, grains, legumes, and oilseeds are all high in niacin. The majority of

39

commercial pet foods contain niacin. In extreme cases, symptoms of deficiencies may involve anorexia or loss of appetite, diarrhea, dermatitis, dementia, stunted growth, damage to soft tissues in the mouth (like necrosis of the tongue), and excessive drooling. Toxins can cause convulsions and blood in the feces, but this is uncommon.

Pantothenic Acid Is a Type of Vitamin B. (B5)

Pantothenic acid aids in fat, protein, and carbohydrate metabolism, as well as other biological functions (B5). It is required for energy production. Fish, fish liver and heart, rice and wheat bran, alfalfa, peanut meal, and yeast contain the highest amounts of this compound found in all foods. The majority of the calcium added to pet food is pantothenate. Even though deficiencies are uncommon, they can lead to heart problems, immune system decline, and weight loss. Dogs have no toxicity levels, but high doses can cause gastrointestinal distress.

Cobalamin B12 (B12)

Cobalamin is the most important and complicated of the B vitamins (B12). It is essential for cell function and influences the metabolism of many physiological systems in dogs, including folate metabolism.

Cobalamin can be produced by a variety of bacteria. Plants contain a small amount of vitamin B12. Meat and a few dairy products are high in iron. Although they are uncommon, deficits can result in neurological problems, growth retardation, and anemia. A lack of vitamin B12 may develop over time if certain vegetable-based diets are regularly followed. Although canine toxins are unknown, they have the potential to cause abnormal reflexes and other neurological conditions.

Vitamin B6 (B9)

Folic acid stimulates DNA synthesis and purine metabolism (vitamin B9). Folic acid is found in liver, egg yolks, and green vegetables; however, heat, freezing, and water storage can make it unstable or destroy it. Symptoms of deficiencies include a loss of appetite, difficulty maintaining or gaining weight, a weakened immune system response, and blood disorders (anemia, clotting issues). Some medications (sulfa drugs) may be difficult to absorb. There is no evidence of canine toxicity.

Biotin (B7) The body of a dog uses biotin to aid in the metabolism of fats, sugars, and amino acids (B7 or H). Many foods contain biotin, albeit in trace amounts. Biotin is found in the highest concentrations in oil seeds, egg yolks, alfalfa meal, liver, yeast, and oil seeds. Biotin supplements are commonly used in commercial pet foods.

Dogs can develop deficiencies from eating raw egg whites and some antimicrobials, but these are uncommon. The biotin in raw egg whites may bind to them, rendering it unavailable to a dog's body. Biotin deficiency can result in keratin synthesis, dermatitis, hair loss, dull coats, and dull skin. There may be signs of delayed growth as well as neurological issues. Toxins that exist are unknown.

Choline

This vitamin is found in cell membranes and helps to reduce fat absorption in the liver. It also plays an important role in clotting, inflammation, and various other body functions. The liver of dogs can produce choline. While it is not a true vitamin by definition, it is necessary and is frequently added to many diets. For all life stages, AAFCO recommends 1,200 mg/kg DM.

Egg yolks, glandular meals, and fish are the best animal sources of choline. The best sources of choline in plants are cereal germs, legumes, and oilseed meals. Insufficient choline levels can lead to the development of fatty livers, extended clotting times, growth impairment, renal issues, and reduced appetite or anorexia. Toxicities aren't known in dogs, but all-natural fats contain choline. Lecithin is an emulsifying agent in foods that is often ingested in most foods.

CHAPTER 5
PREPARATIONS, TOOLS, AND STORAGE OF DOG FOOD

Preparing Homemade Dog Food

Homemade dog food can certainly be a healthy diet for your pet. However, creating a home-cooked meal for your dog may not be the easiest. When you don't do it properly, you could cause your dog a life-threatening nutrient deficiency. Making food at home is the only way for you to know for sure what goes into your dog's meal and how it is prepared. With homemade dog food, you can use fresh, human-grade ingredients. You can even include supplements that help your dog's overall health.

Be Careful

While there are great benefits to a homemade pet food diet, you still need to be careful. You can't simply look up recipes on the internet since these may not be nutritionally well-balanced. This is why you need to take your meal preparation seriously. So before you switch to a homemade dog food diet, you should know three things.

Talk with a Professional

The most important thing you can do is talk with an expert before switching to a homemade diet. They can evaluate your dog's medical history and get their help in creating recipes that meet all of your dog's nutritional needs. As with humans, all dogs are different, and each has its own unique nutritional needs based on a range of factors, including the following:

- Age
- Weight
- Activity Level
- Breed
- Health Condition(s)

To make these decisions yourself you would need to do a lot of research. As we've discussed, each dog has their own needs when it comes to protein, carbohydrates, fat, vitamins, and minerals. It is also important because you will need to change based on your dog's changing nutritional needs over time. This is why you need to work with a professional when it comes to creating a homemade dog food diet.

Homemade Diets Aren't Long-Term

Most homemade dog food diets are created for a specific reason. They are used to meet the nutritional needs of puppies, seniors, or dogs with specific health conditions. There are specific recipes for a variety of specific needs. Many of these recipes aren't recommended to be fed to a dog in the long term. You may need to add supplements to make the recipe balanced nutritionally, or you may need to feed a variety of recipes to give your dog all they require. Just make sure you adjust the diet as needed, and if you need to switch back to a commercial diet then be prepared to do so.

Homemade Diets are Just a Starting Point

Once you have a list of recipes in mind for your pet, take it to a professional and have them adjust it as needed for your pet. They may recommend adding additional supplements and/or ingredients based on your pet's individual needs. So when it comes to putting together a diet for your dog, let's look at what goes into preparing these recipes.

Complete and Balanced Recipes

A homemade dog food diet must be complete and balanced. This means it needs to meet all of your dog's nutritional needs. Homemade dog food diets include a wide range of foods that rely on balance over time, rather than balance in every meal. Similar to how humans eat, a dog that gets everything they need within a week or two of meals will have a diet that is complete and balanced.

Guidelines for Creating Recipes

When it comes to making a recipe for your dog, there are some guidelines you should follow. For example, you should use a single type of food, such as chicken to make up more than half of the diet. Unless specified, homemade dog food recipes can be either raw or cooked. Human food leftovers can be included as long as they are safe human foods. Let's look at some of the guidelines to follow when creating your own dog food recipes.

Deciding to add one or two homemade meals to your dog's weekly diet to give him some variety is not too hard to do. However, switching to a completely homemade diet is not a change to be taken lightly. Our dogs need balanced nutrition that can help them live their best life; trying to figure that balance out week in and week out can certainly be challenging for pet parents. Once you have tried some of these recipes out on your dog, you might decide to make your dog's principal diet to be homemade. Set up an appointment with your veterinarian to discuss the best way to make the diet switches for your dog. The vet will be able to suggest foods and supplements for your dog's size, age, and activity level, as well as look into any other health concerns.

The stage of life that your dog is in will help to determine the formulation of a proper diet. Puppies need a higher fat, calorie, and protein content in their food compared to adult dogs.

The size of a dog will also help to determine the dog's specific needs; large breed pups do not require as much calcium in their diet as their smaller cousins. Even having too many nutritional elements can lead to health problems. Below is some food to consider for your dog.

Too much protein in your dog's diet can cause their liver and kidneys to overwork as they try to remove the excess protein the dog's body is unable to absorb. Some puppies can experience growth problems when they do not have enough protein in their diet.

If your pup's diet has too much fat included in it, this can lead to excess poundage on your pup. On the other hand, too little fat in their diet can lead to a dull coat and flaky skin.

If your dog has too many vitamins included in their diet, this could stress your dog's organs and even lead to bladder stones, while a lack of vitamins can make your dog feel tired and weak.

In a balanced diet for your dog fiber plays an important role. The presence of an abundance of fiber in your dog's diet can cause the production of excess gas. Not enough fiber can lead to loose stools. There are many factors involved in finding the right balance—then that is when you will discover the significant benefits. You can make your dog's diet suit its taste and work with your veterinarian to ensure it gets all it needs to keep healthy.

A human knows that eating processed foods or fast foods can harm one's health.

The same can be applied to dogs. You may have tried to feed your dog a variety of dishes, from dry foods to wet foods, raw foods to premade foods. However, you wonder if making your dog food yourself is a better alternative to grabbing the nearest dog food off the counter at the grocery store.

Being in control of the ingredients and quality of your dog's food comes with many benefits. While premade foods can be saviors in terms of time, you don't truly want what your dog is consuming. You don't know if your dog is getting full nutritional benefits or is simply getting stuff with high calories, chemicals, additives, and preservatives that normally come with processed foods.

So, making the dog's meal yourself helps you know exactly what your poodle's food consists of. Also, it gives you control over the preparation of those meals. You can equally assess the quality of ingredients that go into the preparation of your dog meals and exclude anything unsafe for the dog.

That aside, you probably possess a dog that dislikes commercial foods. Such fussy eaters will require that you feed them something from your pantry. Test out different homemade foods on them till you can create a food plan for them.

Preparing your poodle's meal helps you avoid allergens that can negatively affect your dog while also adapting the food to meet its needs. You can swap certain ingredients and alternate the quantity of the meals to suit your dog's needs.

Fruits and veggies are important components in a dog's diet. They balance the alkaline and acidic levels of your dog's body. When proteins such as meat are often consumed by your dog, its alkaline level will increase. So, giving your dog enough fruits and vegetables will balance out those alkaline levels.

Fruits and vegetables are rich in fiber, carbohydrates, and fats, among others. They provide the much-needed glucose and amino acids your dog needs. Additionally, they are full of vitamins that improve your dog's health by increasing energy, boosting immunity, and preventing cancer.

Last but not least, they aid in the digestion of your dog's food because they contain enzymes that slow down aging, degeneration and improve health.

However, note that not all fruits and veggies are good for your dogs. Vegetables like onions and avocados must be avoided at all costs because they pose a great danger to dogs.

If you want to include fruits and vegetables in your dog's meals, opt for those in season. Those fruits and veggies in season are cheaper compared to off-season fruits. So, save cost, time, and energy by using seasonal foods.

Giving your dog the same old meal gets boring. Spice up your dog's meals with some specialty dishes. Now this will cost more since the quality of ingredients used in making those dishes are top notch.

Homemade dog food can be a nutritious diet for your pet. However, preparing a home-cooked meal for your dog may not be the easiest task. If you don't do it correctly, your dog could suffer from a life-threatening nutrient deficiency. You can only know what goes into your dog's food and how it is prepared if you prepare it yourself. You can use fresh, human-grade ingredients when making homemade dog food. You can also include supplements that will benefit your dog's overall health.

Take Caution

While there are numerous advantages to feeding homemade pet food, you must exercise caution. You can't just look up recipes on the internet because they might not be nutritionally balanced. This is why you must be meticulous in your meal preparation. Before transitioning to a homemade dog food diet, there are three key pieces of information you need to be aware of.

Consult a Professional

Before embarking on a homemade diet, the most important thing you can do is consult with an expert. They can evaluate your dog's medical history and get their help in creating recipes that meet all of your dog's nutritional needs. All dogs, like people, are unique, and each has its own set of nutritional requirements based on a variety of factors, including the following:

- Age • Weight • Activity Level • Breed • Health Status (s)

To make these decisions on your own, you would need to conduct extensive research. As previously stated, each dog has unique protein, carbohydrates, fat, vitamins, and minerals requirements. It is also important because your dog's nutritional needs will change over time, necessitating changes. This is why you should consult with a professional when developing a homemade dog food diet.

Homemade Diets Aren't Sustainable

Most homemade dog food diets are designed with a specific purpose in mind. They are used to meet the nutritional requirements of puppies, senior dogs, and dogs with certain medical conditions. There are recipes for a variety of specific requirements. Many of these recipes should not be fed to a dog regularly. You may need to add supplements to make the recipe nutritionally balanced, or you may need to feed a variety of recipes to provide your dog with everything they require. Just make sure to adjust the diet as needed, and be prepared to return to a commercial diet if necessary.

Diets Made From Scratch Are Only a Starting Point

Once you've compiled a list of recipes for your pet, take it to a professional and have them modify it as needed. Based on your pet's specific needs, they may recommend adding additional supplements and/or ingredients. So, when it comes to creating a diet for your dog, let's take a look at what goes into making these recipes.

Recipes That Are Complete and Balanced

A complete and balanced homemade dog food diet is essential. This means it must meet all of your dog's nutritional requirements. Homemade dog food diets include a diverse range of foods that rely on long-term balance rather than the balance at each meal. A dog who gets everything they need within a week or two of meals will have a complete and balanced diet, similar to how humans eat.

Recipe Development Guidelines

You should follow some guidelines when creating a recipe for your dog. For example, a single type of food, such as chicken, should account for more than half of the diet. Unless otherwise specified, homemade dog food recipes can be raw or cooked. Human food leftovers are acceptable as long as they are safe. Let's take a look at some of the rules to remember when making your own dog food recipes.

Adding one or two homemade meals to your dog's weekly diet to give him variety is simple; however, switching to a completely homemade diet is not something to be taken lightly. Our dogs require balanced nutrition to help them live their best lives; however, figuring out that balance week in and week out can be difficult for pet parents. After experimenting with some of these recipes on your dog, you may decide to make homemade food your dog's primary diet. Make an appointment with your veterinarian to discuss the best way to transition your dog's diet. The veterinarian will be able to recommend foods and supplements based on your dog's size, age, and activity level and investigate any other health concerns.

The stage of life in which your dog is will aid in the formulation of an appropriate diet. Puppies require more fat, calories, and protein in their food than adult dogs.

A dog's size will also help determine its specific needs; large-breed puppies do not require as much calcium in their diet as their smaller cousins. Even having too many nutritional elements can cause health issues. Here are some dog foods to consider:

Too much protein in your dog's diet can overwork their liver and kidneys as they try to remove the excess protein that the dog's body is unable to absorb. Some puppies may experience growth problems if they do not consume enough protein.

If your pup's diet contains an excessive amount of fat, he or she may gain weight. On the other hand, a lack of fat in their diet can result in a dull coat and flaky skin.

Too many vitamins in your dog's diet can stress their organs and even lead to bladder stones, whereas a lack of vitamins can make your dog tired and weak.

Fiber is an important part of your dog's balanced diet. An excessive amount of dietary fiber for your canine may result in gas. The absence of sufficient fiber can contribute to the development of loose stools. Finding the right balance involves several factors, and it is only after that that you will notice the significant benefits. You can tailor your dog's diet to his preferences and work with your veterinarian to ensure he gets everything he needs to stay healthy.

A person understands that eating processed foods or fast foods can be harmful to one's health.

The same is true for dogs. You may have tried feeding your dog a variety of foods, including dry foods, wet foods, raw foods, and premade foods. However, you wonder if making your dog food is a better option than grabbing the nearest dog food off the shelf at the grocery store.

Controlling the ingredients and quality of your dog's food has numerous advantages. While ready-made foods can save time, you don't necessarily want what your dog is eating. You don't know if your dog is getting all of the nutritional benefits or if he is just getting the high-calorie, chemical, additives, and preservatives that come with processed foods.

Making the dog's food yourself allows you to know exactly what your poodle's food is made of. It also gives you control over how those meals are prepared. You can also assess the quality of ingredients used in preparing your dog's meals and eliminate anything harmful to the dog.

Aside from that, you most likely have a dog who dislikes commercial foods. Such picky eaters will necessitate feeding them something from your pantry. Try out various homemade foods on them until you can develop a food plan for them.

Preparing your poodle's meal allows you to avoid allergens that can harm your dog while also adapting the food to meet its specific needs. You can change the ingredients and the amount of food to suit your dog's needs.

Fruits and vegetables are essential components of a dog's diet. They keep your dog's alkaline and acidic levels in check. When your dog consumes proteins such as meat regularly, his alkaline level rises. Giving your dog enough fruits and vegetables will help to balance his alkaline levels.

Fruits and vegetables contain fiber, carbohydrates, and fats, among other nutrients. They provide your dog with the necessary glucose and amino acids. Furthermore, they are high in vitamins, which improve your dog's health by increasing energy, boosting immunity, and preventing cancer.

Last but not least, they help your dog's digestion because they contain enzymes that slow aging, degeneration, and improve health.

Nonetheless, it is important to note that not all fruits and vegetables should be fed to your dogs. Vegetables such as onions and avocados should be avoided at all costs because they are extremely dangerous to dogs.

If you want to feed your dog fruits and vegetables, choose those that are in season. As a result, in-season fruits and vegetables are more readily available and less expensive than out-of-season fruits. So, use on-season foods to save money, time, and energy.

Giving your dog the same old meal becomes tedious. Specialty dishes can help to spice up your dog's meals. This will now cost more because the ingredients used to make those dishes are of the highest quality.

However, make it a point to include one or more of such meals periodically. That will improve the quality of health, vitality, and energy levels of your dog.

Making Canned Dog Food

If you enjoy canning food, you could make some meat and gravy for your pet. It will take time, but it is a great option for long-term storage.

You have the option of canning cooked meat with gravy as well as their entire meal. Canning necessitates the use of a pressure canner, and different meats necessitate different methods. You'll also need canning jars with the appropriate lids.

Canned dog food recipes can be stored on a shelf or in the pantry for many months before they expire if canned safely and properly. It might be best to do it this way for those of you who enjoy this type of thing.

Not to mention that if you take the time now to make the canned food, you will save time later when you may not have as much free time. Follow all of the canning instructions exactly. The majority of pressure canners come with an instruction manual that is jam-packed with useful information.

Appliances and Tools

Now we will go over everything you will need in the kitchen. We'll also have charts to help break down all of the information needed for balanced meals and portions.

You'll need some basic kitchen tools to make these recipes, but if you're already capable of preparing simple meals for yourself, you probably have most of what you need.

Chopping Board

Cutting boards are useful for all types of cooking. I like colored, flexible cutting boards because I can color code them to avoid cross-contamination (for example, red for meats and green for veggies). They also make it simple to transfer chopped food into a pan or a bowl.

Strainer With Fine Mesh

A fine mesh strainer is ideal for rinsing quinoa or rice and removing fat from meat. I prefer one that hangs over the sink because it allows me to pour scalding water through it into the sink in a very controlled manner.

Trays for Ice Cubes

These are ideal for making bite-sized frozen treats. I recommend silicone trays because they make it very easy to remove frozen treats without them breaking. Silicone trays are available in a variety of sizes and shapes.

Food Processor or Immersion Blender

It's more versatile, smaller, and easier to clean than a food processor. However, a food processor does the job and can be very useful, especially if you are cooking in large quantities. There is no need for both; either will suffice.

Knives for the Kitchen (High Quality)

High-quality kitchen knives make a huge difference, but they can be quite expensive. However, purchasing an entire set isn't the only way to go; you can also build as you go. When you feel the weight of a well-balanced, razor-sharp, high-quality knife, you'll realize how much effort and time you've been wasting with dull knives.

Multicookers

These are also known as pasta pots or multicookers (not to be confused with pressure cookers or instant pots). You can steam vegetables over rice in this pot. The benefit is that any nutrients that leach out of the vegetables are absorbed by the rice. It will also include a strainer lid for draining pasta, and having fewer pots means less cleanup, which is always a plus!

Stacking Mixing Bowls

Nesting mixing bowls are always useful. They fit together perfectly, maximizing space efficiency. If you get a set with lids, they can also be used as storage containers.

Pans and Pots

A good set of nonstick or stainless steel pots and pans is a must-have in any kitchen. You will almost certainly use them every day for years. They could be the only set you ever buy if properly cared for. Many different styles are available, so if you don't already have a set, choose the one that best suits you.

Pan for Roasting

A roasting pan is nice, but other baking pans with racks to keep meat and bones out of drippings and fat will do the same. Choose the appropriate size for you.

The Rolling Pin

The treat recipes call for the creation of a dough that must be rolled flat. Various materials and styles are available; choose the one that allows you to roll dough flat.

Hand Mixer vs. Stand Mixer

All of the dessert recipes call for a stand mixer, and a couple of the main courses use it to shred pulled chicken. A hand mixer will also work, so you can make do if that's all you have. A stand mixer is another tool that, if properly maintained, will last a lifetime. They are useful for various recipes, and attachments are available to convert them into a machine suitable for various types of specialty cooking.

Basket for Steaming

Steaming vegetables helps to keep their nutrients from evaporating. Because boiling vegetables removes many of their nutrients, steaming is a better option. Use the attached steamer basket if you have a multicooker. You can also purchase one separately.

Stockpot

Stockpots are ideal for large portions because they have enough space to simmer a large amount of ingredients while keeping the splattering or splashing contained within the deep walls. For the best results, choose one with a heavy bottom.

Storage Containers

Because some meals just keep getting better as leftovers, you probably already have a set of airtight containers. You should have a variety of container sizes to meet your needs.

Utensils

A wooden spoon, spatula, and rice paddle are all useful kitchen tools. These are the tools you'll use every time you cook, no matter what you cook, so they're a must.

Rice Cooker

If you have the space, a rice cooker is a useful addition to your kitchen. It makes it nearly impossible to burn your rice and frees up stovetop space. Many of them also function as steamers (though I don't believe they're meant to be used simultaneously).

The Slow Cooker

Slow cookers are extremely useful for making bone broth. I'd rather leave a slow cooker on for 16 hours than a pot on the stove's back burner. It's not a tool you'll use every day, but it's useful to have when the task calls for it.

The Vacuum Sealer

This is useful for storing food. Freezing single portions is the most efficient way to work and will keep your food fresh. Freeze portions separately, then return to the refrigerator every couple of days to thaw before feeding.

Many of these items will already be in your kitchen. The ones that aren't, well, they have so many uses that you'll wonder how you ever lived without them once you have them.

A vacuum sealer is a good investment if you regularly cook for your dog. It allows you to measure out and freeze individual servings.

Bulk-cooking multiple meals over the weekend and storing them in the freezer means you can take out a few meals at a time to thaw. The cooking process then feels like a well-oiled machine and less like you're scrambling to make dinner for even more mouths every day.

How to Store Homemade Dog Food

Storing homemade dog food is similar to storing any other type of food. I usually make large batches and freeze the majority of them. It's critical to use an airtight container or freezer bag. Frozen dog food can be stored for a month or more, but it's important to check to make sure it hasn't become freezer-burned.

If food is properly cared for, it can be stored for a longer period. As a result, it can be kept all year, regardless of the season or climate. There are several methods for protecting and extending the shelf life of your dog's food.

The primary reason for storing food at home is to ensure quick, medium, and long-term access to meals. Each type of food has different food storage requirements.

Physical, biochemical, chemical, and biological changes and pest infestation cause food to spoil. Bacteria, yeast, and mold are frequently the causes of spoilage. They cause food to spoil, ferment, or mold. Pathogenic microorganisms produce substances that are harmful to humans even when the food is not spoiled. Germs multiply at different rates depending on the food's temperature, water activity, pH level, and oxygen content. The germ content of the food and the temperature at which it was stored are the most important considerations.

Storage for the Short Term: Refrigerator

Fresh, perishable food should be stored at temperatures ranging from 0°C (32°F) to 14°C (57°F). A traditional refrigerator keeps food at temperatures ranging from 4°C (39°F) to 8°C (46°F), while a multi-zone refrigerator keeps food at nearly 0°C (32°F). Bacterial growth is slowed, and enzymatic and chemical spoilage is delayed at these temperatures. The ideal refrigerator storage temperature for most meals is near the freezing point. Meat and fish can be stored for an extended period at temperatures around -2°C (28°F).

Basic refrigerator storage guidelines:

- Purchase fresh foods as frequently as possible.
- As soon as you finish shopping, put everything in the refrigerator. When going shopping, always bring a cooler bag!
- It is critical to keep your goods properly packed. The container keeps food from drying out and changing flavor.
- Store fish and meat in the lower section of the refrigerator, place dairy products on the upper shelves, allocate the top shelf for cheese and leftovers, and reserve the vegetable compartment for fruits and vegetables.

Freezer for Medium-term Storage

Freezing food for several months is an excellent way to save money while retaining nutrients with little discernible loss in quality. Low temperatures and reduced water activity aid in the prevention of microorganism multiplication. Remember that microorganisms do not die when frozen; rather, they resume reproducing once defrosted. Fat oxidation and enzymatic breakdown processes continue to occur in the freezer, albeit much slower. Even when frozen, fat goes rancid.

Freezer Guidelines for preserving aroma, nutrients, and quality:

- Before freezing fruits and vegetables, clean, wash, peel and/or core, chop, and blanch to preserve vitamins and color.
- Freeze just-right portions for consumption.
- Food should be packed in as airtight a container as possible.
- Create labels with the contents' name and date.
- The shelf life of fruit and vegetables ranges from 11 to 15 months, while beef and poultry can last for 9 to 12 months, and fish and high-fat meat for 6 to 9 months.

These items should not be kept in the freezer: eggs, lettuce, fresh salad, radishes, raw potatoes, cucumbers, tomatoes, watermelons, and whole raw apples and pears are all options. Water-rich foods become mushy when frozen. Dairy products should also not be stored in the freezer.

Pantry for Long-term Storage

Long-term storage of preserved and dry food is possible in pantries at temperatures ranging from 15°C (59°F) to 20°C (68°F), in a dry and dark environment. A pantry should be as close to the kitchen as possible, and it should have good ventilation.

The kitchen is not a good storage area due to the high humidity and temperature. Only supplies that will be consumed quickly should be kept here. However, in apartment complexes, it is usually the only place to keep food.

Regular maintenance and careful storage reduce storage losses and spoilage:

- Check the expiration date on food before opening or consuming it.
- Prioritize arranging new supplies towards the back of the shelf and ensure that you utilize the oldest ones before anything else.
- Place opened packages into containers that fit snugly, whether they are made of glass, metal, or plastic.
- Write the name and date on the preserved food.
- Avoid eating food from a can (tin) with a bulging bottom or lid, or from a jar that is no longer airtight.

Preserved foods, flour, salt, sugar, whole canned (tinned) foods, and dry products such as rice, pasta, or cereals should be kept in storage cupboards.

Storage of Dry Dog Food

This is an excellent choice for serving throughout the day because it does not spoil quickly. Dogs enjoy crunching on fresh kibble, but an open bag can quickly become stale or rancid if improperly stored. Consider the following recommendations for storing dry dog food:

Dry kibble should be stored in its original bag inside an airtight plastic, glass, or aluminum container.

Choose pet food storage containers with a rubber gasket to keep moisture and air out. These containers will keep air, humidity, and pests out of the food.

Keeping the food in its original container adds an extra layer of protection and ensures that it tastes good. It also prevents the taste of the container from transferring to the food.

Food should not be stored outside due to temperature fluctuations and the threat of pests such as insects, rodents, and other animals. Food should ideally be stored indoors at 22°Celsius or lower.

You should use a bag of dry food within six weeks for maximum flavor and freshness, and always check the "best by" date to ensure it is still good.

Canine Food Storage

Look for dents, swelling, and/or punctures in the cans that could indicate spoilage or botulism.

Throw away any suspect cans. When disposing of suspect cans, wrap the can in plastic and place it in the trash. When handling, thoroughly wash your hands or use disposable gloves.

Pet food cans should be kept indoors at temperatures no higher than 22°Celsius. Unopened cans need not be refrigerated, and most dogs prefer canned food at room temperature.

Preserve the flavor by storing leftover wet food in the original can with a topper or plastic wrap or put it in an airtight glass container. Leftover canned food can be stored in the refrigerator for up to four days. Choose not to refrigerate it, but rather envelop single-serving portions with plastic wrap and place them in the freezer for three months.

Canine Treats

Treats are an excellent way to spoil your pet if they are fresh and tasty. To do so, follow these steps:

Opened bags of treats should be stored in their original packaging in an airtight container or resealable plastic bag.

Keep treats at temperatures below 22°Celsius.

Most treats are packaged in resealable bags to keep them fresh, which is particularly important for soft treats. To maintain maximum freshness, store freshly baked treats in the refrigerator in a resealable bag or container.

Storage of Raw Diet

If you feed a raw diet, you should take some special precautions when storing it. Raw meat can easily go rancid at room temperature, so keep it in the fridge for no more than four days at a time in a covered container.

When preparing food in bulk, use resealable plastic bags or freezer-safe containers to store it in the freezer. Frozen food can be kept for up to six months if it is kept away from freezer burn.

Raw food must be consumed in one sitting. Leftovers must be picked up right away and stored in the refrigerator. Raw meat should not be left out at room temperature for more than two hours.

Because raw meat is likely to spoil, it should not be served in time feeders.

After handling any type of raw meat, always thoroughly wash your hands.

Now that we know how to prepare a homemade dog food diet, let's help you get started. Consider the following recipes to help you get the framework started for making a homemade dog food diet.

I trust you're enjoying the book! Scan the QR code below to share your thoughts and claim your exclusive bonus!

CHAPTER 6
100 RECIPES

BASIC RECIPES

Prepar. Time　　Cooking Time　　Dog breed　　Difficulty Level

1 SOUTH PACIFIC HOT DOGS

10 minutes   20 minutes   Chihuahua   Easy

Ingredients:

1 pound lean ground turkey, chicken or beef
1 carrot finely grated
1 small sweet potato, cooked and mashed
2 tbsp parsley, finley chopped (optional for extra flavor and digestive benefits)
½ pineapple, peeled, cored, diced, and drained

Directions:

1. Preheat oven to 350°F.
2. Mix all ingredients in a large bowl until well combined. The mixture should be uniform and stick together easily.
3. Shape the mixture into hot dog-like shapes or small sausages that would be an appropriate size for your dog. If the mixture is too sticky to handle, you can wet your hands with a bit of water to make the shaping easier.
4. Place the shaped "hot dogs" on a parchment-lined baking sheet, ensuring they don't touch each other.
5. Bake in the preheated oven for about 20-25 minutes.
6. Let them cool completely before serving to your dog.
7. Pineapple can be a good solution if your dog suffers from coprophagia—eating his own or other dogs' feces. Although most dogs like to eat pineapple, it is not appealing to the dog the second time around, and it can help break this diffi-cult habit.

NUTRITION:

Calories: 170 kcal; Fat: 16 g; Protein: 8 g; Carbohydrates: 4 g.

2 PAMPERED POOCH RICE AND LAMB CASSEROLE

10 minutes | 37 minutes | Beagle | Medium

Directions:

1. Mix rice and safflower oil in a pot over medium heat; mix and cook for 2 minutes.
2. Add the dog-safe broth and ground thyme. Cover, and cook 15 minutes more over medium hotness or until fluid is assimilated.
3. In the interim, cook the ground sheep in a large skillet over medium hotness until seared, around 10 minutes.
4. Then, the channel mixes into the rice alongside the grated dry pressed cottage cheese until the cheddar liquefies. Cool totally before serving.

Ingredients:

1 ½ cup converted long-grain white rice
2 tsp safflower oil
2 cups water
¼ tsp ground thyme
1 cup grated dry pressed cottage cheese
2 cups dog-safe broth
1 pound lean ground lamb

NUTRITION:

Calories: 420 kcal; Fat: 22 g; Carbs: 38 g; Protein: 40 g.

3 STOMACH FRIENDLY KIBBLE

20 minutes | 45 minutes | Dachshund | Easy

Ingredients:

3 cups cooked rice
3 cups rolled oats
2 cups rice flour
2 tbsp bone meal
3 cups homemade broth
1 cup silken tofu, pureed
½ cup olive oil

Directions:

1. Mix the dry ingredients in a mixing cup and then add the broth.
2. Preheat the oven to 200°F (95°C).
3. Pat the mixture onto a baking tray with a thickness of ½ inches (1.2cm). Bake for 45 minutes.
4. Allow to cool slightly, and cut or break into small pieces.
5. Refrigerate for up to 7 days or freeze for up to 6 months.

NUTRITION:

Calories: 300; Fat: 12 g; Protein: 10 g; Carbohydrates: 30 g.

4 CHUCK AND BARLEY STEW

10 minutes | 1 hour 30 minutes | Dachshund | Easy

Directions:

1. Get a stockpot and add the meat, potatoes, celery, and carrots.
2. Add the water to the ingredients.
3. Set a timer for one hour and cook at a high temperature.
4. The barley should be added to the boiling mixture after an hour.
5. Cook for a further 30 minutes.
6. Cool thoroughly before serving a routine-sized quantity.
7. Refrigerate or freeze leftover food and use it as required.

Ingredients:

1 lb. Chopped chuck beef
1 lb. Pearl barley
2 lb. Chopped potatoes
2 lb. Chopped carrots
½ bunch celery, chopped
4 qt. water

NUTRITION:

Calories: 300; Fat: 12 g; Protein: 20 g; Carbohydrates: 28 g.

5 RICE WITH BEEF AND FISH

20 minutes | 20 minutes | Dachshund | Medium

Ingredients:

4 lbs. (1800 g) ground beef
1 sweet potato
3 cups cooked white rice
1 can of mackerel, drained
4 cups peas & carrots
6 eggs
6 egg shells
1 tbsp rosemary, finely chopped
1 tbsp ginger, finely chopped

Directions:

1. Preheat the oven to 350°F (180°C). Brown the ground beef in a pan and drain all of the grease.
2. Pierce sweet potato with a fork and microwave for 10 minutes or until soft.
3. Bake eggshells in the oven for 10 minutes. When done, blend or mash until they form a powder.
4. Steam veggies and then mash with the rosemary and ginger.
5. Add all ingredients into the pan and heat all ingredients.

NUTRITION:

Calories: 400; Fat: 15 g; Protein: 30 g; Carbohydrates: 30 g.

BAKED RECIPES

6 BACON GRAVY

5 minutes | 15 minutes | Shetland Sheepdog | Medium

Ingredients:

6 bacon slices
2 cups milk
2 tsp all-purpose flour

Directions:

1. In a large pan, fry the bacon over medium heat until crisp. Remove the bacon from the pan and break it into little pieces.
2. Remove the bacon fat from the pan and add 2 tbsps back to it.
3. Add the flour to the grease and stir continually. Pour in the milk and constantly whisk while the gravy thickens, lowering the heat after a minute. Stir in the bacon chunks. Simmer until the desired thickness is reached.
4. Use up to one tbsp as a meal topping. Refrigerate for up to 3 days or freeze for up to 6 months in an airtight container.

NUTRITION:

Calories: 200; Fat: 10 g; Protein: 8 g; Carbohydrates: 15 g.

7   CHEESE BISCUITS

10 minutes   15 minutes   Golden Retriever   Easy

Directions:

1. Preheat oven to 375°F.
2. Run the cheese through a grater. Allow it to stay until it gets to room temperature. Add softened margarine and flour to the cheese. Add the milk, and mix until it's a ball
3. Put in the freezer for half an hour.
4. Sprinkle some flour into a wooden board. Cut the cheese into different shapes
5. Set the cut cheese into a baking pan, and bake for 15 minutes until it's brown and firm.

Ingredients:

6 cups of flour
2 ¼ cups of cheddar cheese
1 tbsp Unsalted butter or unsalted margarine
1 cup milk

NUTRITION:

Calories: 150; Fat: 8 g; Carbs: 20 g; Protein: 7 g.

8 CRUNCHY APPLE CUPCAKES

10 minutes | 25 minutes | Chihuahua | Hard

Ingredients:

2-3 cups water
¼ cup applesauce
2 tbsp honey
⅛ tbsp vanilla extract
1 medium egg
4 cups whole wheat flour or oats
1 cup dried apple chips
1 tbsp baking powder

Directions:

1. Mix everything into a dough.
2. Cut into pieces or desired shapes.
3. Bake for 25 minutes.

NUTRITION:

Calories: 100; Fat: 3 g; Protein: 4 g; Carbohydrates: 15 g.

9 DOGGIE BAGELS

10 minutes | 30 minutes | Bulldog | Medium

Directions:

1. Heat your oven.
2. In a glass bowl, mix the wheat with yeast. Pour in the chicken broth and add the honey. Mix well. Gently add the leftover flour.
3. Use the rolling pin to knead the mixture.
4. Ensure the mixed flour is properly covered. It will rise because of the yeast.
5. Divide the mixed flour into 20 pieces, and roll into a ball.
6. Use your finger or the base of a spoon to make a hole.
7. Line the baking pan, and oil it.
8. Place each roll on the pan and allow it to rise.
9. Then bake and allow to cool before serving.

Ingredients:

1 cup wheat flour
1 tbsp chicken broth
2 cups plain flour
1 tbsp yeast
1 tbsp honey

NUTRITION: (1 TARTLET)

Calories: 150; Fat: 2 g; Carbs: 20 g; Protein: 5 g.

10 LIVER GRAVY

10 minutes | 15 minutes | Dachshund | Easy

Ingredients:

1 tbsp olive oil
1 lb chicken liver, washed
1 gallon (3.8l) chicken broth

Directions:

1. Cook liver in oil in a large skillet over medium-high heat until golden.
2. Remove the liver from the heat and purée it in a blender. Pour in the chicken broth. Pulse until smooth.
3. Refrigerate for up to 3 days or freeze for up to 6 months in an airtight container.

NUTRITION:

Calories: 100; Fat: 5 g; Protein: 5 g; Carbohydrates: 1 g.

11 DOGGY COOKIES

10 minutes | 30 minutes | Greyhound | Easy

Directions:

1. Heat your oven to 350°F (175°C).
2. Mix all ingredients into a bowl.
3. Line the baking tray with a cookie sheet. Spread the mixture into the tray.
4. Form small portions of the mix to create each cookie. Bake for 20-30 minutes.

Ingredients:

1 tbsp baking powder
½ cup of cornmeal
4 cups flour
1 tbsp olive oil
1 beaten egg
1 tbsp chicken or beef broth
½ cup steamed carrots
½ cooked chicken or turkey 1 cup mashed potatoes

NUTRITION:

Calories: 100; Fat: 4 g; Carbs: 12 g; Protein: 5 g.

NO-BAKE RECIPES

12 RAW VEGGIE CUPCAKES

10 minutes | 0 minutes | Shetland Sheepdog | Hard

Directions:

1. Wash and trim all vegetables. (Other options include asparagus, broccoli, cauliflower, collards, cabbage, cucumbers, squash, sweet potatoes, and zucchini.)
2. Chop into squares and add to a food processor or blender, 1 cup at a time, to purée, adding water to the mixture as needed.
3. Once all vegetables are puréed, combine all into one mix. Freeze in ice cube trays or small cupcake holders.
4. To serve, remove from freezer and thaw to room temperature (or serve as a frozen treat).
5. Unlocking Those Nutrients
6. Puréeing vegetables breaks down the cellulose wall of the plants. Dogs can't digest cellulose, so puréeing makes the nutrients within the walls available to the dog.

NUTRITION:

Calories: 140 kcal; Fat: 13 g; Protein: 2 g; Carbohydrates: 5 g.

Ingredients:

1 head celery, trimmed
1 bundle carrots, trimmed
1 bunch parsley, trimmed
1 bunch of kale, spinach greens, bok choy, mustard greens, or Romaine lettuce
2 cups Water

13 RAW VEGGIE AND FRUIT TREAT

15 minutes | 0 minutes | Dachshund | Easy

Ingredients:

1 cup raw pumpkin, grated
1/2 cup apples, cored and grated (do not include seeds, as they can be harmful)
1/4 cup blueberries
1/4 cup plain yogurt (low in fat and without added sugars or sweeteners)

Directions:

1. Ensure all fruits and vegetables are thoroughly washed. Grate the pumpkin, carrots, and apples using a box grater or food processor. Remove any apple seeds, as they are toxic to dogs.
2. In a large bowl, combine the grated pumpkin, carrots, apples, blueberries, and ground flaxseed. Mix until the ingredients are evenly distributed.
3. Add the plain yogurt to the mixture and stir until all the ingredients are coated and well combined. The yogurt will help bind the ingredients slightly and add moisture.
4. Using a spoon or your hands, form small bite-sized balls or patties from the mixture. The size should be appropriate for your dog's size and breed.
5. Place the formed treats on a tray lined with parchment paper and refrigerate for at least an hour to firm up slightly and make them more cohesive.
6. Offer these treats to your dog as a fresh, healthy snack. Remember, these are supplementary treats, so they should not constitute the majority of your dog's diet.

NUTRITION:

Calories: 250 kcal; Fat: 6 g; Carbohydrates 50 g; Protein: 12 g.

14   TUNA CASSEROLE

10 minutes | 0 minutes | Shetland Sheepdog | Easy

Directions:

1. Drain tuna, reserving the tuna water to use in place of water in a treat recipe.
2. Mix tuna, pasta, peas, parsley, and cheese in a medium bowl. Serve.
3. Refrigerate unused portions. Refrigerate for 3 days or freeze in an airtight container for up to 3 months.

Ingredients:

1 (9-ounce) can tuna packed in water
1 cup cooked pasta, drained
½ cup frozen peas, thawed
¼ cup chopped fresh parsley
¼ cup grated parmesan cheese

NUTRITION:

Calories: 200; Fat: 8 g; Carbs: 20 g; Protein: 22 g.

15 DEHYDRATED SWEET POTATO CHEWS

10 minutes | 0 minutes | Rottweiler | Medium

Ingredients:

2 medium sweet potatoes

Directions:

1. Wash and peel the sweet potatoes, carefully removing any sprouts or green spots.
2. Slice the potatoes lengthwise no thinner than ¼" thickness. If you cut slightly thicker slices, your dog will experience a chewier consistency; however, it's important to note that these slices may dry out faster and have a shorter shelf life, even if stored in the refrigerator.
3. Arrange the slices on the dehydrating trays. Ensure that the slices don't touch each other; otherwise, the edges won't dry correctly.
4. The potatoes should be dried for roughly 14 hours, but keep in mind that different dehydrators may require different time lengths.
5. Cool and refrigerate. Refrigerate for up to 1 week or freeze in an airtight container for up to 6 months.

NUTRITION:

Calories: 250; Fat: 1 g; Carbs: 40 g; Protein: 1 g.

16 TAPIOCA AND TOFU

10 minutes | 0 minutes | Chihuahua | Easy

Directions:

1. Tapioca should be cooked as directed on the box, using salt in water to prevent the starch from sticking.
2. Allow the tapioca to cool completely.
3. Finely chop the tofu and mix it with the tapioca that has been left to cool.
4. Serve a portion. Keep any leftovers in the fridge.

Ingredients:

10.5 oz. Plain tofu
1 cup tapioca
¼ tsp salt

NUTRITION:

Calories: 250; Total Fat: 8 g; Total Carbs: 10 g; Protein: 5 g.

BREAKFAST RECIPES

17 SPINACH OMELET

10 minutes | 5 minutes | Beagle | Easy

Directions:

1. In a small bowl, beat the eggs, then add spinach and cheese. Pour into a nonstick skillet coated with cooking spray.
2. Cook over medium heat until partially set, about 5 minutes, then flip with a spatula to cook to the desired doneness. Cool before serving. Refrigerate unused portions for up to 3 days.

Ingredients:

2 eggs
1 cup baby spinach leaves, torn
1 tbsp grated Parmesan cheese

NUTRITION:

Calories: 180 kcal; Carbohydrates: 2 g; Protein: 15 g; Fat: 12 g.

18 HOMEMADE BREAKFAST FOR DOGS

10 minutes | 10 minutes | Shetland Sheepdog | Medium

Ingredients:

1 or 2 eggs
5-10 baby spinach leaves
1 tbsp sprinkle of dried kelp

Directions:

1. Begin by frying the eggs.
2. Chop the spinach.
3. Remove the egg and allow it to cool.
4. Fry the spinach for about 15 seconds, then add it to the eggs.
5. Sprinkle a little kelp on the eggs.
6. Serve!

NUTRITION:

Calories: 150 kcal; Fat: 12 g; Carbs: 2 g; Protein: 10 g.

19 LIVER CORN BREAD

10 minutes | 30 minutes | Shetland Sheepdog | Hard

Directions:

1. Preheat oven to 350°F. Grease a cookie sheet with at least a ½" edge.
2. In a blender, purée the liver. Pour liver into a large mixing bowl. Add corn muffin mix and egg. Stir until just combined, then pour the batter onto the cookie sheet.
3. Bake for 30 minutes.
4. Cool before slicing, then refrigerate. Refrigerate for up to 3 days or freeze in an airtight container for up to 6 months.

Ingredients:

1 lb beef or chicken liver, rinsed
1 (8.5-ounce) box corn muffin mix
1 egg

NUTRITION:

Calories: 230; Total Fat: 10 g; Carbohydrates 22 g; Protein: 16 g.

20 CHEESY EGGS AND RICE

10 minutes | 30 minutes | Dachshund | Easy

Ingredients:

6 scrambled eggs
½ cup cottage cheese
1 cup cooked brown rice

Directions:

1. Mix ingredients and cook together.

NUTRITION:

Calories: 250; Fat: 10 g; Carbs: 20 g; Protein: 20 g.

21 HOMEMADE DOG FRENCH OMELET

10 minutes | 30 minutes | Poodle | Medium

Directions:

1. Add a little olive oil.
2. Before adding to the pan, whisk the eggs.
3. Cook lightly before including the peppers and salmon.
4. Fold the egg until it is cooked through. Remove from the heat and allow it to cool before serving.

Ingredients:

½ cup sliced grilled salmon fillet
2 eggs
½ green pepper, diced
1 tbsp. Olive oil

NUTRITION:

Calories: 250; Fat: 15 g; Carbs: 5 g; Protein: 20 g.

22 PEANUT BUTTER OATMEAL

10 minutes | 30 minutes | Shetland Sheepdog | Easy

Ingredients:

1 cup steel-cut oats
1 cup blueberries
1 cup all-natural peanut butter
1 tbsp coconut oil

Directions:

1. Oats should be softened by cooking them.
2. Peanut butter and coconut oil should be heated in the microwave until they are less sticky.
3. Put everything together and serve!

NUTRITION:

Calories: 350; Fat: 20 g; Carbs: 40 g; Protein: 12 g.

23 PUMPKIN & BERRY OATMEAL

10 minutes | 0 minutes | Poodle | Easy

Directions:

1. Soften the oats in a pot of water until they are mushy.
2. Remove stems from spinach leaves and chop finely
3. Stir together all of the ingredients.
4. Serve!

Ingredients:

2 cups steel-cut oats
¼ cup pumpkin puree
¼ cup blueberries
¼ cup chopped spinach
3 cups Water

NUTRITION:

Calories: 300; Fat: 7 g; Carbs: 40 g; Protein: 10 g.

24 COTTAGE CHEESE BREAKFAST

10 minutes | 0 minutes | Chihuahua | Medium

Ingredients:

⅓ cup cottage cheese
⅓ cup plain yogurt
⅓ cup mashed blueberries

Directions:

1. Mix all ingredients in a medium bowl and serve. If you have a small dog and only need a portion of this dish, you can store the remainder in the refrigerator for up to 5 days.
2. Along with blueberries, other good options for this easy breakfast include puréed or finely chopped apples (discarding the core and seeds), puréed carrots, bananas, mashed blackberries, and other favorite fruits and vegetables your dog enjoys.

NUTRITION:

Calories: 100; Fat: 2 g; Carbs: 10 g; Protein: 5 g.

25 BAKED EGGS MUFFINS

15 minutes | 30 minutes | Dachshund | Hard

Directions:

1. Preheat the oven to 350°F (180°C). Fill muffin tins (small size) with parchment paper or grease them.
2. Whisk together the eggs, cottage cheese, baking soda, cheese, chicken, and tuna in a big mixing bowl.
3. Fill each cup with the egg mixture and bake for 30 minutes or until firm.
4. Allow cooling before serving. Refrigerate egg muffins for up to three days.

Ingredients:

12 eggs
½ cup of cottage cheese
½ tsp powdered baking soda
1 cup cheddar cheese, shredded
½ cup cooked shredded chicken
1 can tuna (5 oz./140 g) in water, drained

NUTRITION:

Calories: 100; Fat: 7 g; Carbs: 2 g; Protein: 8 g.

26 CHIA SEED OATMEAL

10 minutes | 0 minutes | Shetland Sheepdog | Easy

Ingredients:

1 cup almond milk
1 cup unsweetened oats
2 apples
2 tsp chia seeds
2 tbsp honey
1 tsp lemon extract
1 cup plain Greek yogurt (low-fat)

Directions:

1. Combine the almond milk, oats, and chia seeds in a mixing bowl.
2. After removing the core, mix the grated apples, honey, and lemon juice. Make certain that the apple seeds don't come into contact with your dog's mouth. Combine the chia seed and oats with the apples and yogurt.
3. Combine all ingredients in a large mixing bowl and thoroughly mix. Cover and chill overnight. Let the chia seeds sit for at least 12 hours to make sure they are ready. Store for up to five days in the refrigerator.

NUTRITION:

Calories: 250; Fat: 6 g; Protein: 10 g; Carbohydrates: 38 g.

27 FISHERMEN'S EGGS

10 minutes | 15 minutes | Dachshund | Easy

Directions:

1. Preheat oven to 375°F. Coat an oven-safe 8" × 8" casserole dish with nonstick spray.
2. Drain sardines (reserve water for another recipe or a tasty topping for your dog's food). Chop sardines and mix with parsley.
3. Line the prepared dish with the sardine mixture, then top with eggs. (Either beat the eggs and pour over the sardines or crack each egg individually on a different portion of the mixture.)
4. Bake until eggs are cooked to the desired doneness, about 15 minutes.
5. Cool before serving to your dog. Refrigerate for 3 days or freeze in an airtight container for up to 6 months.

NUTRITION:

Calories: 200; Fat: 10 g; Carbs: 2 g; Protein: 15 g.

Ingredients:

1 (3.75-ounce) can of sardines in water
2 tbsps fresh parsley
4 eggs

BEEF BASED RECIPES

28   TURMERIC BEEF

10 minutes | 30 minutes | Beagle | Medium

Directions:

1. Cook beef thoroughly.
2. Cook rice until it is soft.
3. Heat the broccoli.
4. Add all ingredients to the rice.

Ingredients:

2 pounds beef
1 pound broccoli
1 cup white rice
¼ cup turmeric powder
2 tbsp coconut oil

NUTRITION:

Calories: 400; Fat: 16 g; Protein: 24 g; Carbohydrates: 28 g.

29 GROUND MEAT LOAF

10 minutes | 30 minutes | Poodle | Easy

Ingredients:

2 pounds of ground meat sauteed in olive oil
1 cup cooked brown rice
4 boiled eggs
1 package cauliflower
1 package chopped carrots
4 tbsp low-fat cottage cheese
2 tbsp bone meal

Directions:

1. Cook together everything except the vegetables.
2. Add vegetables and cook for another ten minutes.
3. Stir and serve or store as desired.

NUTRITION:

Calories: 380; Fat: 18 g; Carbs: 20 g; Protein: 24 g.

30 BEEF AND SWEET POTATO STEW

10 minutes | 30 minutes | Shetland Sheepdog | Hard

Directions:

1. Bake the sweet potato and set aside to cool.
2. Dice the stew meat and cook in a skillet with vegetable oil on medium heat.
3. Dice the sweet potato.
4. Remove the beef and set aside.
5. Add water and flour to the beef fat in the skillet and stir until gravy forms.
6. Add vegetables and beef to the gravy and mix well.
7. Cook until vegetables are tender.
8. Cool before serving a meal and store leftovers.

Ingredients:

1 pound beef stew meat
½ cup carrots
1 sweet potato
½ cup green beans
½ cup flour
½ cup water
1 tbsp vegetable oil

NUTRITION:

Calories: 300; Carbohydrates: 28 g; Protein: 20 g; Fat: 12 g.

31 GROUND BEEF HOMESTYLE DINNER

Ingredients:

1 cup ground beef
½ cup of beef kidney
¼ cup kale
½ cup yellow squash

Directions:

1. Boil everything separately.
2. Combine ingredients.
3. Add a cup of uncooked oatmeal if desired.

NUTRITION:

Calories: 300; Fat: 16 g; Carbs: 18 g; Protein: 20 g.

32 CABBAGE BEEFY SALAD

10 minutes | 0 minutes | Shetland Sheepdog | Easy

Directions:

1. Mix egg yolk with the remaining ingredients. Leave out the potatoes and cabbage.
2. Arrange cabbage and potatoes in a bowl. Arrange the beef.
3. Pour the egg yolk dressing into the salad.

Ingredients:

1 tbsp parsley
1 cup cooked potatoes
1 cup cooked beef
1 cup shredded cabbage
¼ cup of vinegar
4 eggs yolk
1 tbsp Dijon mustard
1 tbsp Olive oil

NUTRITION:

Calories: 300; Carbohydrates: 18 g; Protein: 22 g; Fat: 20 g.

33 BEEF FRIED RICE

10 minutes | 40 minutes | Dachshund | Easy

Ingredients:

2 cups water
1 cup uncooked jasmine rice
2 eggs
1 pound lean ground beef
½ cup sliced celery
1 tbsp sesame oil
½ cup frozen chopped carrots and peas

Directions:

1. In a medium saucepan, bring water to a boil over high heat. Once boiling, add the rice and stir.
2. Return the pot to a boil, then lower the heat to low, cover, and simmer the rice until tender and all the water is absorbed for about 18-25 minutes.
3. Fluff with a fork and set aside.
4. Spray a large skillet with nonstick cooking spray and heat over medium heat.
5. Beat eggs in a small bowl, then pour into skillet and cook until firm.
6. Remove from heat and slice eggs into strips.
7. Combine eggs with rice and set aside; return skillet to stove.
8. Spray the skillet again if needed. Cook ground beef and celery over medium heat until beef is thoroughly cooked (about 10 minutes), stirring to prevent sticking and over-browning.
9. Pour sesame oil over the beef mixture.
10. Add carrots and peas, cooked rice, and cooked egg strips, constantly stirring for 3-4 minutes to thoroughly combine and warm the ingredients.
11. Cool dog's portion before serving.
12. Refrigerate for 3-4 days or freeze in an airtight container for up to 3 months.

NUTRITION:

Calories: 320; Fat: 12 g; Carbs: 30 g; Protein: g.

34 BEEF STEW

10 minutes | 22 minutes | Shetland Sheepdog | Easy

Directions:

1. Pan-fry the beef until well done, and drain off the oil from the pan
2. Use a fork to prick the sweet potato and microwave for 2 minutes at 50% power.
3. Cook the peas and carrots until they are tender.
4. Simmer for approximately 20 minutes, occasionally stirring, with enough water to cover the ingredients.
5. Allow cooling before serving!

Ingredients:

1 ½ lb beef- any kind
1 sweet potato
½ cup carrots
½ cup frozen peas
2 tbsp coconut oil
1 cup water

NUTRITION:

Calories: 280; Carbohydrates: 20 g; Protein: 20 g; Fat: 10 g.

FISH BASED RECIPES

35 PARSLEY FISH & OREGANO

10 minutes | 30 minutes | Dachshund | Hard

Directions:

1. Pierce sweet potato with a fork and microwave for 10 minutes or until soft.
2. Steam green beans until soft.
3. Bake fish according to package directions.
4. Add all ingredients together and serve!

Ingredients:

4 pounds white fish
1 sweet potato
½ lb green beans
4 tbsp oregano
4 tbsp parsley
2 tbsp olive oil

NUTRITION:

Calories: 220; Fat: 8 g; Carbs: 18 g; Protein: 21 g.

36 RICE AND SALMON

10 minutes | 30 minutes | Beagle | Easy

Ingredients:

¼ cup brown rice
0.33 lb (150 grams) salmon (or sardines)
1/3 cup cauliflower
1 pinch parsley
1 tbsp sunflower oil

Directions:

1. Clean the rice and boil it in plenty of water.
2. Cut the salmon into small cubes and cut the cauliflower.
3. Then sauté the salmon and vegetables, sprinkling the parsley on the top.
4. When your rice is done cooking and you have lightly cooked the salmon and vegetables, mix in with the rice and prepare to serve.
5. Add a small quantity of vegetable oil, mix, and cool.

NUTRITION:

Calories: 240; Fat: 8 g; Carbs: 21 g; Protein: 18 g.

37 VEGETABLE/FISH PATTIES

10 minutes | 8 minutes | Chihuahua | Medium

Directions:

1. Drain and fry the salmon with the flour and eggs.
2. Remove the patties from the oil.
3. Stir the vegetables in the oil for 5 to 8 minutes.
4. Mix and set aside to cool.
5. Serve or store as desired.

Ingredients:

2 cans salmon
2 potatoes
2 carrots
2 cooked eggs
2 celery stalks
5 tbsp flour
1 tbsp oil

NUTRITION:

Calories: 150; Fat: 8 g; Carbs: 12 g; Protein: 16 g.

38 FISH HOMESTYLE DINNER

10 minutes | 30 minutes | Shetland Sheepdog | Easy

Ingredients:

2 pounds of fish fillets
1 or 2 cans of pink salmon
3 cups diced vegetables
1 cup cooked brown rice or other grain

Directions:

1. Cook fish and vegetables separately.
2. Mix.
3. Allow cooling.
4. Serve or store as desired.

NUTRITION:

Calories: 180; Carbohydrates: 13 g; Protein: 22 g; Fat: 7 g.

39 SALMON BALLS

8 minutes | 15 minutes | Golden Retriever | Easy

Directions:

1. Preheat oven to 350° F. Grease lightly on a baking sheet.
2. In a mixing bowl, mix all the ingredients. Using a melon baller or spoon, scoop the mixture, and roll it into balls. Place balls on the baking sheet.
3. Bake the salmon balls for about 15 minutes. Allow the salmon balls to cool before serving them to your dog. Store in the fridge for 3-4 days or in an airtight container; freeze them for up to 6 months.

Ingredients:

1 egg
1 tbsp olive oil
1 cup cooked brown rice
½ cup cooked salmon, chopped

NUTRITION:

Calories: 150; Fat: 6 g; Carbs: 8 g; Protein: 6 g.

40 SALMON AND SPINACH HASH

10 minutes | 30 minutes | Shetland Sheepdog | Hard

Ingredients:

1 tsp olive oil
1 (7.5-ounce) can salmon, drained
1 cup frozen spinach, thawed
4 eggs

Directions:

1. Heat olive oil in a medium skillet over medium-high heat. Add salmon and spinach, stirring until completely heated.
2. Add eggs and scramble.
3. Cool before serving.
4. Refrigerate for up to 3 days.

NUTRITION:

Calories: 160; Fat: 10 g; Carbs: 2 g; Protein: 14 g.

41 APPETIZING SEA FOOD

10 minutes 30 minutes Shetland Sheepdog Medium

Directions:

1. Clean the squid.
2. Pour some fish stock into a pot, add butter, squid, and boil.
3. Serve the cooked squid with rice.

Ingredients:

1 cup boiled rice
1 tbsp butter or margarine
1 tbsp fish stock
1 tbsp fresh squid

NUTRITION:

Calories: 240; Fat: 8 g; Carbs: 38 g; Protein: 12 g.

42 TUNA BALLS

10 minutes | 30 minutes | Beagle | Easy

Ingredients:

2 oz canned tuna
1 cup rice
4 eggs
½ lb spinach
Optional coconut oil and breadcrumbs

Directions:

1. Cook the rice until it is tender.
2. Cook the eggs and spinach in the rice, occasionally stirring until the eggs are set and the spinach has wilted.
3. Mix everything.
4. If the mixture is too dry, add a couple of tsp of coconut oil. If your pup's stomach can tolerate it, add a couple of tbsp of breadcrumbs.
5. Form into balls and chill, or store as a mixture in the refrigerator.

NUTRITION:

Calories: 240; Fat: 10 g; Carbs: 18 g; Protein: 22 g.

CHICKEN BASED RECIPES

43 HOMEMADE CHICKEN BROTH

5 minutes | 60 minutes | Chihuahua | Easy

Ingredients:

1 chicken (3 lb. /1360 g)
1 cup water

Directions:

1. Cover chicken in a large stockpot with 3" (7.5cm) of water.
2. Bring to a boil, then simmer for 1 hour.
3. Remove chicken from the water and reserve for another recipe.
4. For the safety of your dogs, it is important to dispose of any cooked chicken bones as they can pose a risk of splintering and choking.
5. If you want to remove the fat, keep the liquid refrigerated. The fat will rise to the top of the liquid when it is cold
6. It can be frozen in ice cube trays or plastic zip-top bags.
7. Chicken broth is a delectable frozen treat that may be used in many recipes.

NUTRITION:

Calories: 50; Carbs: 1 g; Protein: 2 g; Fat: 1 g.

44 CHICKEN RISOTTO

10 minutes | 30 minutes | Chihuahua | Medium

Directions:

1. Bring the 2 eggs to a boil in a pot and remove them once they are fully cooked.
2. Grate the boiled eggs with a grater. Crush the shells of the eggs in another bowl.
3. Cut the chicken into small cubes.
4. Bring another pot of water to a boil until it boils.
5. In a pot, sauté the asparagus and add rice and some boiling water.
6. Stir the asparagus and rice constantly to avoid sticking.
7. Add water every time the rice absorbs it. Once it is practically done, add the chicken pieces and the grated egg.
8. To finish, don't forget to add ½ yogurt and crushed eggshells.

NUTRITION:

Calories: 180; Fat: 8 g; Carbs: 14 g; Protein: 18 g.

Ingredients:

0.33 lb (150 grams) chicken or turkey meat
1/8 cup white rice
2 eggs
½ yogurt
¼ cup of asparagus
1 tbsp corn vegetable oil
1 cup chicken stock (or souper cubes)
1 cup Water

45 BASIC CHICKEN WITH RICE

10 minutes | 30 minutes | Shetland Sheepdog | Easy

Ingredients:

2 cups chicken broth or bone broth
1 cup cooked chicken
1 cup white rice
2 cups water

Directions:

1. Combine all ingredients in a large saucepan.
2. Over high heat, bring to a boil.
3. Reduce to a simmer, cover the pan, and cook until the rice is puffy.
4. Cool completely before serving, and refrigerate leftovers.

NUTRITION:

Calories: 190; Carbs: 24 g; Protein: 18 g; Fat: 6 g.

46 CHICKEN CASSEROLE

10 minutes | 15 minutes | Chihuahua | Medium

Directions:

1. Remove the excess amount of fat from chicken breasts before cutting them into small chunks.
2. Over medium heat, heat a non-stick skillet and cook chicken breasts until they are no longer pink.
3. Bring chicken broth, vegetables, and chicken to a boil in a large pot. Let simmer for about 12-15 minutes or until the carrots have become tender.
4. Let cool before serving.
5. Note: The leftover portion can be refrigerated for up to five days; if the chicken breasts become stuck to the skillet, try frying in a small amount of olive oil.

Ingredients:

4 chicken breasts
½ cup carrots, chopped
½ cup oats, rolled
½ cup beans, green, chopped
4 cups chicken broth, unsalted
½ cup broccoli, chopped

NUTRITION:

Calories: 220; Fat: 6 g; Carbs: 18 g; Protein: 22 g.

47 POULTRY PALOOZA

10 minutes | 25 minutes | Shetland Sheepdog | Hard

Ingredients:

1 tbsp canola oil
3 ½ lb boneless, skinless chicken thighs, diced into bite-size bits
1 lb chicken gizzards, chopped
1 lb. of chicken hearts, chopped
½ cup chopped chicken livers, about 3 oz.
1 tbsp finely chopped fresh rosemary
1 cup water
2 ½ tsp Eggshell Powder

Directions:

1. Prepare the oil in a big stockpot by heating it over medium-low heat.
2. After adding the chicken thighs, gizzards, hearts, and livers, as well as the rosemary, and water, continue to boil the mixture for 20-25 minutes or until all of the meat turns brown and is fully cooked.
3. After removing the pot from the heat, wait until the stew has cooled down before adding the eggshell powder.

NUTRITION:

Calories: 220 ; Carbs: 12 g; Protein: 35 g; Fat: 12 g.

48 CHICKEN THIGHS AND TABBOULEH

10 minutes

30 minutes

Shetland Sheepdog

Easy

Directions:

1. Put the stock into a large stockpot and bring it up to a boil.
2. After weighing the bulgur wheat, place it in a big bowl and pour the boiling liquid into it.
3. Cover and let the mixture settle for one hour. The bulgur will become fluffy and light when it has absorbed all of the stock.
4. While the stock is simmering, bring the oil to temperature in the same stock pot you used for the stock over a heat setting between medium and high.
5. After adding the chicken and bell pepper to the stockpot, stir the contents of the pot regularly for about eight minutes or until the chicken is fully cooked and the bell pepper has become more tender.
6. Take the saucepan off the heat and then add the parsley to it.
7. After adding the chicken mixture to the bulgur, give everything a quick stir to ensure that everything is well combined. Wait until the mixture has cooled down before adding any supplements.

Ingredients:

1 cup chicken stock
1 cup bulgur wheat
¼ cup canola or olive oil
2 lb of boneless, skinless chicken thighs, cut into 1-inch dice
1 medium red bell pepper that is seeded and cut into 1-inch dice
½ cup chopped fresh parsley or mint

NUTRITION:

Calories: 340; Carbs: 20 g; Protein: 22 g; Fat: 18 g.

49 CHICKEN AND CHEESE MEA

10 minutes 30 minutes Beagle Easy

Ingredients:

3 cups cooked chicken
3 cups cooked desired grains
3 cups cottage cheese
1 ½ cup cooked broccoli
1 ½ cup cooked squash

Directions:

1. Cook together grains, cheese, and chicken.
2. Add vegetables just before done and cook for another ten minutes.
3. Stir and serve or store as desired.

NUTRITION:

Calories: 400; Carbs: 32 g; Protein: 28 g; Fat: 25 g.

50 CHICKEN AND VEGETABLE MEDLEY

10 minutes | 15 minutes | Shetland Sheepdog | Medium

Directions:

1. In a large skillet, heat olive oil over medium heat. Add the chicken and then cook for a minimum of 5 minutes.
2. Add the brown rice and vegetable medley. Cook for approximately 8-10 minutes, thoroughly mixing.
3. Add in the parsley, gently mixing, and remove from heat.
4. Let cool completely before serving.
5. Place any leftovers in the refrigerator.

Ingredients:

3 chicken breasts, cubed
1 egg
2 cups vegetable medley, frozen
2 cups brown rice, cooked
1 tbsp olive oil
3 tbsp parsley, chopped

NUTRITION:

Calories: 380; Fat: 12 g; Carbs: 38 g; Protein: 27 g.

51 TURKEY GRAVY

10 minutes | 5 minutes | Shetland Sheepdog | Easy

Ingredients:

2 cups pan drippings
¼ cup all-purpose flour
¼ cup water

Directions:

1. Remove fat from the drippings by cooling the drippings and then skimming the fat from the top. Reserve ¼ cup of the fat for use in this recipe.
2. Heat the ¼ cup fat in a large skillet and add flour over medium-high heat.
3. Stir constantly for about 1 minute to brown the flour. Pour in turkey drippings and water, stirring constantly, and reduce to desired thickness.
4. Cool completely before serving to dogs. Use a spoonful as a meal topper. Refrigerate for up to 3 days or freeze in an airtight container for up to 6 months.

NUTRITION:

Calories: 120; Carbs: 10 g; Protein: 2 g; Fat: 6 g.

52 TURKEY AND VEGETABLES

10 minutes | 30 minutes | German Shepherd | Hard

Directions:

1. Cook meat until almost done.
2. Add vegetables and cook for another ten minutes.
3. Stir and serve or store as desired.

Ingredients:

2 pounds of turkey meat
2 cups cooked grains of choice
1 cup green beans
1 cup carrots
½ cup water
2 tbsp vegetable oil

NUTRITION:

Calories: 320; Fat: 16 g; Carbs: 22 g; Protein: 30 g.

53 CHICKEN & SWEET POTATO

10 minutes   5 hours   Poodle   Medium

Ingredients:

2 pounds of chicken breast
½ cup chopped carrots
2 tbsp olive oil
1 sweet potato cut into chunks
1 cup rice
½ cup chopped green beans
1 tbsp rosemary, optional

Directions:

1. Put all the ingredients in a crock pot and simmer on high heat for 5 hours, or until the chicken is cooked thoroughly and everything is mushy.

NUTRITION:

Calories: 360; Fat: 11 g; Carbs: 32 g; Protein: 30 g.

SLOWCOOKER RECIPES

54. EASY SLOW BEEF AND BEANS

15 minutes | 6 hours | Beagle | Easy

Ingredients:

2 ½ lbs (1100 g) ground beef
1 (15 oz./400 g) can kidney beans, rinsed and drained
1 ½ cup butternut squash in small cubes
1 ½ cup carrots, finely chopped
¾ cup peas, fresh or frozen
4 cups water

Directions:

1. In a large mixing basin, combine all of the ingredients.
2. Place the mixture in a slow cooker.
3. Pour in 4 cups of water and cook on low for 6 hours.
4. Let it cool before serving or storing it in the refrigerator.
5. Refrigerate for 3 days or freeze for up to 6 months in an airtight container.

NUTRITION:

Calories: 350; Fat: 16 g; Carbs: 31 g; Protein: 33 g.

55 SLOW BEEF AND TURKEY

20 minutes | 10 hours | Dachshund | Medium

Directions:

1. Combine the beef and turkey in a slow cooker.
2. Using an electric hand mixer, fully mix the eggs, including the shells, until they are completely combined. The shells will break down into tiny fragments. Pour this mixture on over the meat.
3. Add the spices, fruit, and vegetables to the slow cooker and mix.
4. Cook on low for 10 hours or more.
5. Let it cool before serving or storing it in the refrigerator. Refrigerate for 3 days or freeze for up to 6 months in an airtight container.

Ingredients:

1 lb (450 g) ground beef
1 lb (450 g) turkey ground
2 carrots, big
1 lb (450 g) of sweet potato
1 potato
1 cup broccoli florets
1 cup cauliflower florets
1 apple
2 eggs
1 tbsp flax seed, ground
1 tbsp of parsley
1 tsp turmeric powder
1 tsp ginger powder
1 tsp of cinnamon

NUTRITION:

Calories. 300; Fat: 10 g; Carbs: 18 g; Protein: 21 g.

56 SLOW-COOKED CHICKEN AND BARLEY

- 10 minutes
- 8 hours
- Labrador Retriever
- Easy

Ingredients:

2 ½ cups pearl barley
2 lb boneless, skinless chicken thighs, diced
2 cups finely chopped green beans
2 large carrots, diced or shredded
1 cup water
2 tbsp canola oil

Directions:

1. Put all of the ingredients into the saucepan of a slow cooker with a capacity of 6 qt., give it a good stir to incorporate everything, and make sure everything is distributed evenly.
2. Cook for 8 hours with the temperature set to a low setting.
3. The stew should be allowed to cool down before any more ingredients are added, after which the cooker should be turned off.

NUTRITION:

Calories: 400; Fat: 14 g; Carbs: 40 g; Protein: 33g.

57 SLOW CHICKEN

10 minutes | 12 hours | Shetland Sheepdog | Easy

Directions:

1. Fill a 4-quart (4-liter) slow cooker halfway with water and add all of the ingredients.
2. Cook for 12 hours or more on low.
3. Let it cool before serving or storing it in the refrigerator. Refrigerate for 3 days or freeze for up to 6 months in an airtight container.

Ingredients:

1 cup brown rice, uncooked
3 chicken breasts, boneless and skinless
2 carrots, peeled and cut into rounds
1 cubed sweet potato (unpeeled but with any green parts removed)
½ cup cranberries
1 cup water

NUTRITION:

Calories: 300; Fat: 5 g; Carbs: 32 g; Protein: 23 g.

58 BROTHSICLES

10 minutes | 8 hours | Shetland Sheepdog | Medium

Ingredients:

12 cups water
1 pound chicken meat

Directions:

1. Add water and chicken meat to a 4-quart (or larger) slow cooker.
2. Cook chicken on low overnight in the slow cooker, for at least 8 hours. If using whole chicken parts, remove the bones and skin from the mix and discard.
3. When done, shred any large pieces and return the chicken to the slow cooker.
4. Stir the mixture. Ladle the broth mixture into plastic cups or ice cube trays. The chicken will settle to the bottom of the broth, so stir between each Brothsicle so each frozen treat includes bits of chicken.
5. Freeze overnight. Store in a zip-top plastic bag in the freezer for up to 6 months when frozen.

NUTRITION:

Calories: 120; Fat: 4 g; Carbs: 2 g; Protein: 12 g.

PASTRIES & SPECIAL OCCASION RECIPES

59 VALENTINE'S DAY RED BELL PEPPER COOKIES

30 minutes | 30 minutes | Beagle | Medium

Ingredients:

1 red bell pepper (½ oz./15 g)
¼ cup chicken broth (homemade)
2 eggs
1 tbsp plain low-fat yogurt
2 tbsp extra-virgin olive oil
3 ½ cups rice flour
½ cup cooked chicken, crumbled
1 cup carrots, minced

Directions:

1. Preheat the oven to 350°F. Prepare a baking tray.
2. Remove the red bell peppers' stem, core, and seeds. Dice the flesh into small pieces.
3. Combine flour, broth, eggs, yogurt, and olive oil in a large mixing bowl. Toss in the chicken and vegetables. Combine thoroughly.
4. Using a spoon, scoop out golf ball-sized balls from the dough. Spread out and flatten with the back of a fork on an uncooked baking tray. Bake for 30 minutes.
5. Allow cooling on a drying rack before refrigerating. Refrigerate for 3 days or freeze for up to 6 months in an airtight container.

NUTRITION:

Calories: 150; Total Fat: 5 g; Carbs: 22 g; Protein: 6 g.

60 BIRTHDAY BLUEBERRY CUPCAKES

10 minutes   20 minutes   Beagle   Hard

Directions:

1. Turn the oven temperature up to 350 ° F.
2. Ground the kibble into coarse flour in a food processor or blender.
3. After grinding, measure out ½ cup.
4. Mix the ground kibble, flour and baking powder. in a large bowl until everything is properly mixed.
5. Add the wet ingredients: whisk in the eggs and milk or yogurt until the batter is well combined. The consistency should be similar to a slightly gritty cake batter due to the ground kibble.
6. Fold in the blueberries carefully to distribute them evenly throughout the batter.
7. Prepare the muffin tins by greasing them or lining them with a paper baking cup. (Avoid using baking cups made of foil; paper baking cups are digestible, so there's no risk even if your dog mistakenly eats one of them, but foil baking cups might create issues.) When filling the cup with the batter, fill each one half to two-thirds of the way.
8. Bake for 15 to 20 minutes, until the top is brown and golden. (The amount of time required to bake the treats may vary based on the ingredi-ents of the dry dog food that was used and the amount of food that was placed in each baking cup)
9. Take the cupcakes out of the oven, wait for them to cool down complete- ly, and then store them in a container that can keep air out.
10. If you choose, you may top the cake with a layer of whipped cream cheese. You may either include a few blueberries into the icing or add a little bit of ground dog chow on top of each cupcake.

Ingredients:

½ cup high-quality dry dog food kibble
1 cup whole wheat or oat flour
1 tbsp aluminum-free baking powder
1 cup fresh or frozen blueberries
2 large eggs
2/3 cup evaporated low-fat milk or plain yogurt

NUTRITION:

Calories: 150; Total Fat: 6 g; Carbs: 20 g; Protein: 5 g.

61 BIRTHDAY BONES

10 minutes | 20 minutes | Bulldog | Medium

Ingredients:

2 cups whole wheat flour
1 tbsp baking powder
1 cup unsalted natural peanut butter
1 cup skim milk

Directions:

1. Preheat the stove to 375°F. Oil treat sheets. Mix the flour and preparing powder; put away.
2. In a medium bowl, combine the peanut butter and milk. Mix in the flour combination until all around mixed. Turn out the batter onto a delicately floured surface and manipulate until smooth. Carry out to ¼ inch thickness and cut into shapes utilizing dough shapers. Spot 2 inches separated onto the pre-arranged treat sheets.
3. Prepare for 20 minutes on the preheated stove or until daintily brown. Eliminate from treat sheets to cool on wire racks.

NUTRITION:

Calories: 170; Fat: 8 g; Carbs: 20 g; Protein: 10 g.

62 VALENTINE HEARTS

10 minutes | 15 minutes | Shetland Sheepdog | Easy

Directions:

1. Turn the oven temperature up to 350°F.
2. Place all the dry ingredients in a large bowl and stir them until they are well combined.
3. To make a firm dough, begin by adding the eggs, water, food coloring, and vanilla extract one at a time. Gradually stir in the dog-safe chicken broth.
4. Knead the dough for a total of 2 minutes using your hands.
5. Roll the dough into a ball and set it on a breadboard that has been dusted with flour.
6. The dough should be rolled out to a thickness of approximately ¼ inch.
7. Cut out heart shapes using a cookie cutter measuring 2 inches to form the cookies from the rolled-out dough.
8. Put the cookies on a cookie sheet that has been buttered.
9. Bake for up to 15 minutes or until the top is brown and golden.
10. Take the baked goods out of the oven, let them cool completely, and then store them in the refrigerator in an airtight container.

NUTRITION:

Calories: 150 kcal; Fat: 10 g; Carbs: 22 g; Protein: 10 g.

Ingredients:

3 cups all-purpose flour
½ cup non-fat dry milk
½ tsp baking powder
½ tsp salt
½ cup dog-safe chicken broth
2 large eggs
½ cup warm water
1 tsp red food coloring or a red dye alternative (optional)
1 tsp vanilla extract

63. SWEET POTATO POTSTICKERS

30 minutes | 20 minutes | Poodle | Easy

Ingredients:

1 cup sweet potato, cooked (roughly 2 medium sweet potatoes, peeled)
1 tbsp fresh rosemary
⅓ cup of ricotta cheese
1 pack of wonton wrappers
¼ cup grated Parmesan cheese
1 tsp sunflower seed oil

Directions:

1. Preheat the oven to 350°F.
2. Combine the sweet potato, rosemary, and cheese in a blender or food processor. Pulse until well combined.
3. Add 1 tbsp of the sweet potato and cheese stuffing should be placed in the middle of a wonton wrapper; seal the edges with oil to keep them closed. Place the wontons on a baking tray.
4. Sunflower oil should be used to coat the wontons.
5. Bake for 15-20 minutes until golden brown.
6. Cool before serving to your dog or refrigerating. Refrigerate for 3 days or freeze for up to 6 months in an airtight container.

NUTRITION:

Calories: 190 kcal; Fats: 2 g; Carbs: 10 g; Protein: 6 g.

64 POTATO CRANBERRY CHRISTMAS COOKIES

10 minutes | 15 minutes | Great Dane | Medium

Directions:

1. Turn the temperature in the oven up to 350°F.
2. Combine all of the ingredients except the cranberries, and mix well. The dough will be dense and difficult to work with. Drop the half tsp onto cookie sheets that have been buttered. Put a full cranberry in the middle of each cookie and gently press it down so it doesn't move about. This will ensure that the fruit remains in place.
3. Bake for ten to fifteen minutes or until the bottoms are brown and golden.
4. Take it out of the oven, wait until it has cooled completely, and then store it in a container that can keep air out.

Ingredients:

2 cups potato flour
1 cup garbanzo flour
1 cup instant mashed potatoes
1 cup evaporated low-fat milk
½ cup applesauce
2 large eggs
1 cup whole frozen cranberries

NUTRITION:

Calories: 400 kcal; Fats: 20 g; Carbs: 22 g; Protein: 18 g.

65 HALLOWEEN CHICKEN FINGERS

40 minutes | 25 minutes | Poodle | Hard

Ingredients:

1 egg
1 ½ cup cooked chicken
1 tsp powdered baking soda
½ cup whole-wheat flour
2 cups all-purpose flour
1 tbsp molasses
20 almonds (whole)

Directions:

1. Preheat the oven to 350°F.
2. Prepare a baking tray.
3. In a blender, purée the chicken until it resembles baby food, adding a little water if required.
4. Stir in the egg and baking powder.
5. In a medium mixing basin, combine the flours.
6. Combine with the chicken mixture, then knead the dough. Take a golf ball-sized piece of dough and shape it into a 4" (10cm) long tube with your hands. It should be about the same thickness as a finger when you place it on the baking tray.
7. Under the region where the fingernail will be, fill a tiny hole with molasses. Place a single almond on top and gently press it down to secure it. The almond's tip should be pointing outwards, like a spiky fingernail.
8. Bake for 20-25 minutes.
9. Allow to fully cool before serving or storing.
10. Refrigerate for 3 days or freeze for up to 3 months in an airtight container.

NUTRITION:

Calories: 180 kcal; Fats: 8 g; Carbs: 18 g; Protein: 10 g.

RECIPES FOR SENIOR DOGS

66 SENIOR DOGS CHIL

10 minutes | 10 minutes | Beagle | Medium

Ingredients:

2 cooked chicken breasts
½ cup drained kidney beans
½ cup drained black beans
½ cup carrots
2 cups chicken broth

Directions:

1. Mix all ingredients and cook for 10 minutes, then serve or store as desired.

NUTRITION:

Calories: 220 kcal; Fats: 5 g; Carbs: 20 g; Protein: 18 g.

67 CHICKEN COOKIES

10 minutes | 30 minutes | Poodle | Easy

Directions:

1. Preheat your oven to 350°F (175°C).
2. Make the homemade baking mix, combining the flour with baking powder, salt (if using) and oil in a bowl.
3. Mix until the mixture is crumbly.
4. In a large mixing bowl, combine the ground dog kibble, the homemade baking mix previously prepared and the can of chicken soup. Stir until all the ingredients are well-incorporated and you have a consistent dough.
5. Line cookie sheets with parchment paper. You can form small portions of the dough by hand or use cookie cutters to create shapes that your dog will enjoy.
6. Bake until done.
7. Allow the treats to cool completely before serving. Store any leftover as needed.

Ingredients:

2 cup whole wheat flour
1 tbsp aluminum-free baking powder
1/2 tbsp salt (optional)
2 tbsp olive or coconut oil
1 cup ground high-quality dog kibble
1 (18.8 ounces) can of chicken soup

NUTRITION:

Calories: per 220 kcal; Protein: 10 g; Carbs:24 g; Fat: 12 g.

68 BEEF DINNER DELIGHT

10 minutes · 30 minutes · Bulldog · Easy

Ingredients:

2 pounds of ground beef
1 cup cooked grains of choice
1 ½ cup mixed vegetables

Directions:

1. Cook meat and rice together.
2. Add vegetables before things are almost done.
3. Cook for another 10 minutes.
4. Stir and serve or store as desired.

NUTRITION:

Calories: 360 kcal; Fats: 18 g; Carbs: 22 g; Protein: 32 g.

69 SENIOR CHICKEN DINNER

10 minutes | 30 minutes | Dachshund | Hard

Directions:

1. Cook together everything other than vegetables.
2. Once almost done, add vegetables.
3. Cook for another 10 minutes.
4. Stir and serve or store as desired.

Ingredients:

2 cups ground chicken
½ cup chicken liver
1 cup cooked rice
½ cup vegetables
2 cooked eggs
1 tbsp fish oil

NUTRITION:

Calories: 340; Carbs: 26 g; Fat: 18 g; Protein: 28 g.

70 BEAN SOUP

30 minutes | 4 hours | Beagle | Easy

Ingredients:

3 ½ quarts (liters) water
1 pound (450 g / 2 cups) dried navy beans
1 meaty ham bone (1 ½ pound / 600 g)
1 cup cubed potatoes
1 cup thinly sliced celery
1 cup chopped carrots

Directions:

1. Bring 2 ½ quarts (liters) of water to a boil. For 2 minutes, boil the beans; then remove them from the heat and let them stand for 1 hour.
2. Add the ham bone to the beans and simmer for 2 hours or until almost soft.
3. Time to add the potatoes, celery, and carrots. Simmer for 1 more hour.
4. Remove the ham bone, cut away the flesh, dice it, and add it to the beans. Allow cooling to room temperature before serving.
5. Refrigerate for 3 days or freeze for up to 6 months in an airtight container.

NUTRITION:

Calories: 220; Fat: 5 g; Protein: 14 g; Carbohydrates: 31 g.

71 FRUITY CHICKEN SOUP

30 minutes | 3 hours | Chihuahua | Medium

Directions:

1. Place the chicken and water in a large stockpot and cover.
2. Simmer for about 2 ½ hours, until the chicken is cooked through
3. After cooking, remove the chicken from the pot and allow it to cool somewhat. Using your hands, shred the meat into small pieces after removing the skin and bones by pulling it apart.
4. Return the meat to the pot with the broth.
5. Add the chicken broth, celery, carrots, apples, green beans, and parsley, and simmer for 25 minutes.
6. Place the noodles into the pot and allow them to simmer for 8 to 10 minutes, or until they are tender.
7. Let cool to room temperature and serve.
8. Refrigerate for 3 days or freeze for up to 6 months in an airtight container.

NUTRITION:

Calories: 150; Fat: 6 g; Carbs: 15 g; Protein: 12 g.

Ingredients:

3-pound (1300 g) roasting chicken, quartered
2 quarts (liters) water
1 ½ cup homemade chicken broth
2 cups chopped celery
2 cups chopped carrots
2 large apples, chopped
1 cup chopped green beans
¼ cup chopped fresh parsley
4 cups uncooked egg noodles

72 MAX AND PENNY'S SPINACH

20 minutes | 25 minutes | Bulldog | Easy

Ingredients:

2 large eggs
2 tbsp extra virgin olive oil
2 cups cooked brown rice
2 cups fresh sprouting spinach
1 can drained and chopped sardines (8.5oz/240 g)
1 cup Water

Directions:

1. Bring a saucepan of water to a boil over high heat. Add the rice and cook as directed on the package. Typically, this should last for 18-25 minutes, or until cooked and the liquid has been absorbed.
2. In a mixing cup, smash the eggs with a fork. Cook the eggs in a pan over medium heat until firm. Remove the pan from the heat.
3. After removing the eggs from the pan, cut them into thin strips.
4. In a skillet, combine the rice and olive oil over medium heat. Stir constant-ly until the rice is heated, then add the spinach. Cover and simmer until the spinach is completely cooked. Stir in the sardines and eggs until well combined.
5. Allow to cool before serving. Refrigerate for 3 days or freeze for up to 6 months in an airtight container.

NUTRITION:

Calories: 240; Fat: 12 g; Protein: 12 g; Carbohydrates: 16 g.

73 CHICKPEA STEW

10 minutes | 6 hours 10 minutes | Shetland Sheepdog | Medium

Directions:

1. In a large nonstick skillet, heat oil over medium heat. Add carrot and cook until tender, approximately 5 minutes. Stir in brown sugar, ginger. Cook for 1 minute, constantly stirring to prevent sticking. Remove from heat.
2. Place the mixture in a 5-quart slow cooker. Add chickpeas, potato, bell pepper, green beans, and water or stock. Cook on high for 6 hours or until vegetables are fork-tender.
3. Add spinach and coconut milk, stirring until spinach wilts. Cool before serving to the dog. Refrigerate for up to 3 days.
4. Beneficial Beans
5. Like black beans and soybeans, chickpeas help regulate blood sugar in dogs. A source of natural fiber, chickpeas also include many proteins and minerals that boost your dog's immune system.

NUTRITION:

Calories: 360; Fat: 10 g; Carbs: 40 g; Protein: 18 g.

Ingredients:

1 tbsp olive oil
1 cup (¼" -thick) carrot slices
1 tsp brown sugar
1 tsp peeled and grated fresh ginger
3 cups cooked chickpeas
1 ½ cup peeled and cubed baking potato
1 cup diced green bell pepper
1 cup cut green beans
1 ¾ cup water or vegetable stock
3 cups fresh baby spinach
1 cup light coconut milk

74 PUMPKIN BALLS

10 minutes | 15 minutes | Beagle | Hard

Ingredients:

½ cup pumpkin puree
1 cup coconut flour
1 cup quick-cooking oats
1 tbsp coconut oil
1 egg
1 eggshell
1 tbsp honey
¼ cup plain yogurt
¼ cup water

Directions:

1. Preheat the oven to 350°F.
2. Bake the eggshell for seven minutes.
3. Pulverize the eggshells and oats in a food processor until they are a fine powder.
4. Combine all of the ingredients in a large bowl.
5. The mixture can be made into balls, or it can also be used to make muffins
6. Bake for around 15 minutes!

NUTRITION:

Calories: 150; Carbohydrates: 24 g; Protein: 6 g; Fat: 8 g.

75 PUMPKIN RICE

10 minutes | 15 minutes | Rottweiler | Medium

Directions:

1. Bring the vegetables, Pumpkin Purée, and water to a boil in a large saucepan. Stir once or twice while it cooks.
2. Add the rice to the saucepan and return to a boil over medium heat. Reduce the temperature to low and cook for another 5 minutes.
3. Remove from heat and set aside for 10 minutes, until the rice and veggies have absorbed all of the liquid.
4. Allow for complete cooling before serving to your dog. Refrigerate for 3-4 days or freeze for up to 6 months in an airtight container.

Ingredients:

1 tbsp olive oil
1 cup frozen mixed veggies (without onions and garlic)
1 cup pureed pumpkin
2 cups broth (chicken or veggie)
2 cups instant brown rice, uncooked

NUTRITION:

Calories: 250; Fat: 4 g; Carbs: 38 g; Protein: 8 g.

SWEET TREATS

76 PUMPKIN-APPLE DOG TREATS

10 minutes | 15 minutes | Greyhound | Medium

Directions:

1. Preheat the stove to 400°F. Line a preparing sheet with material paper.
2. Spot 4 cups oats in the bowl of a food processor; beat until finely ground. Move to a blending bowl.
3. Mix in ground apple. Blend in canned pumpkin and egg until all around joined; the combination will be thick and marginally tacky.
4. Roll batter on a surface sprinkled with staying ¼ cup oats to a ½-inch thickness. Cut shapes with a cutout and move to the pre-arranged preparation sheet.
5. Prepare in the preheated broiler until fresh and brilliant, 12 to 15 minutes. Eliminate a wire rack to cool totally.

Ingredients:

4 cups rolled oats, or as needed
1 medium apple, cored and grated
1 egg
1 cup canned pumpkin
¼ cup rolled oats

NUTRITION:

Calories: 140; Carbs: 14 g; Fat: 1 g; Protein: 6 g.

77 QUICK AND EASY HOMEMADE DOG TREATS

10 minutes | 30 minutes | Poodle | Hard

Ingredients:

1 ¼ pound ground raw turkey
2 cups whole wheat flour
1 cup instant oatmeal
1 cup grated carrots
2 eggs, beaten
1 tsp olive oil

Directions:

1. Combine one turkey, flour, oats, carrots, eggs, and olive oil in a bowl. Let sit until the fluid has been retained, around 10 minutes.
2. Preheat the broiler to 350°F (175°C). Gently oil two 12-cup biscuit tins.
3. Spoon the turkey combination into the pre-arranged biscuit cups.
4. Heat in the preheated stove until brilliant brown, 15-20 minutes. Let cool on a rack.

NUTRITION:

Calories: 170; Carbs: 18 g; Fat: 6 g; Protein: 12 g.

78 PEANUT BUTTER AND BANANA DOG BISCUITS

10 minutes | 30 minutes | Greyhound | Medium

Directions:

1. Preheat the broiler to 300°F. Gently oil a heating sheet.
2. Mix the egg, peanut butter, banana, and nectar in a medium bowl. Mix in the flour and raw grain; blend well. Turn the mixture out onto a floured board and roll to ¼ inch thick. Cut into wanted shapes with a cutout, place on a pre-arranged heating sheet, and brush tops with egg white.
3. Heat bread rolls in a preheated broiler until dried and brilliant brown, around 30 minutes, contingent upon size. Eliminate from broiler and cool on a wire rack.

Ingredients:

1 egg
⅓ cup peanut butter
½ cup mashed banana
1 tbsp honey
1 cup whole wheat flour
½ cup wheat germ
1 egg white, lightly beaten, for brushing

NUTRITION:

Calories: 160; Carbs: 10 g; Fat: 8 g; Protein: 12 g.

79 ALMOND AND BANANA TREATS

10 minutes | 10 minutes | German Shepherd | Easy

Ingredients:

1 tsp cinnamon, grounded
½ banana
¾ cup almond butter, unsalted
1 egg

Directions:

1. Preheat oven to 350°F. Use parchment paper to line a baking sheet.
2. In a bowl, mash the banana and add the rest of the ingredients.
3. Blend well and spoon onto the parchment paper.
4. Bake for a minimum of 10 minutes.
5. Let cool before serving.

NUTRITION:

Calories: 180; Carbs: 8 g; Fat: 12 g; Protein: 8 g.

80 CAROB DOG BISCUITS

10 minutes | 25 minutes | Great Dane | Medium

Directions:

1. Preheat oven to 350°F.
2. Combine the baking soda, flour, and baking powder in a bowl.
3. Combine the peanut butter, maple syrup, and coconut milk in another bowl.
4. Blend both mixtures and drop by a spoonful onto a baking sheet.
5. Bake for approximately 25 minutes and let cool.
6. In a saucepan, melt the carob chips and coconut oil.
7. Let the carob chips mixture cool. Dip the biscuits into the mixture.
8. Serve the biscuits after they've cooled.

Ingredients:

2 cups coconut flour
1 tbsp coconut oil
1 cup peanut butter, smooth
½ cup carob chips, melted
1 cup coconut milk
1 tbsp maple syrup
1 tsp baking powder
½ tsp baking soda

NUTRITION:

Calories: 300 kcal; Carbs: 20 g; Fat: 18 g; Protein: 8 g.

81 BASIC BAKED CHICKEN TREATS

10 minutes | 12 minutes | Beagle | Easy

Ingredients:

1 (10 oz) can chicken with liquid
2 eggs
1 cup tapioca flour
½ cup white flour
1 tbsp coconut oil

Directions:

1. Preheat the oven to 350°F.
2. Blend chicken and eggs.
3. Pour in a bowl and stir in flour and oil.
4. Spread into the desired mold.
5. Bake for 12 minutes.
6. Once cooled, remove the treats from the mold.
7. Refrigerate or freeze and feed as a treat.

NUTRITION:

Calories: 120; Fat: 4 g; Carbs: 12 g; Protein: 8 g.

82 APPLE CHEDDAR BISCUITS

10 minutes | 30 minutes | Labrador Retriever | Hard

Directions:

1. Preheat the oven to 350°F.
2. Line a baking sheet with parchment paper.
3. Mix all ingredients in a bowl with 3 tbsp of water to form a dough.
4. Roll dough to ¼ inch thick and cut out biscuits.
5. Bake for 30 minutes until brown and firm.
6. Cool on a wire rack in the oven overnight.
7. Store in an air-tight container for up to two weeks.

Ingredients:

2 cups barley flour
½ cup oatmeal
⅓ cup shredded cheddar cheese
¼ cup parmesan cheese
⅓ cup unsweetened applesauce
2 tbsp olive oil
3 tbsp water

NUTRITION:

Calories: 150; Fat: 5 g; Carbs: 15 g; Protein: 17 g.

83 PEANUT BUTTER TREATS

10 minutes | 40 minutes | Golden Retriever | Easy

Ingredients:

1 ½ cup water
2 cups flour (wheat or coconut generally)
1 tbsp natural honey
1 cup rolled oats
1/3 cup all-natural peanut butter
½ tbsp fish oil

Directions:

1. Preheat the oven to 350°F.
2. Mix the flour and oats in a large mixing bowl or basin.
3. Pour in one cup of water and blend until it is smooth.
4. Incorporate the peanut butter, honey, and fish oil into the mixture and blend until all ingredients are fully combined.
5. Gradually incorporate the water until the amalgamation reaches a dense and dough-like texture.
6. Pour flour lightly over a flat surface. Roll the dough onto the flat surface to create a ¼-inch thick sheet.
7. Use a cookie cutter to create shapes. Put the cookies onto a baking tray and cook for 40 minutes. Let them cool completely before feeding.

NUTRITION:

Calories: 180; Total Fat: 6 g; Total Carbs: 18 g; Protein: 8 g.

84 PUMPKIN TREATS

10 minutes | 15 minutes | German Shepherd | Medium

Directions:

1. Heat the oven to 350°F.
2. Blend or whisk ingredients together.
3. Place into the desired pan.
4. Bake for 10 to 15 minutes.

Ingredients:

2 cups coconut flour
½ cup all-natural peanut butter
1 cup pure pumpkin
2 eggs

NUTRITION:

Calories: 140; Total Fat: 6 g; Total Carbs: 15 g; Protein: 8 g.

TRAINING TREATS

85 HOMEMADE DOG TREATS

10 minutes | 20 minutes | Greyhound | Medium

Directions:

1. Preheat the stove to 350°F. Line 2 preparing sheets with material paper.
2. Blend carrots, oats, and apple in a huge bowl. Whisk peanut butter and eggs until completely consolidated in a subsequent bowl. Fill the oat blend and mix until wholly joined.
3. Drop ½ tbsp of hitter onto the pre-arranged heating sheets. Level each treat with your hands until they are ½-inch thick.
4. Prepare in the preheated broiler until treats are firm to the touch and start to brown in the last 15–20 minutes. Permit to cool a couple of moments on the preparing sheets before eliminating to a wire rack to cool totally.

Ingredients:

1 ¼ cup grated carrots
1 ¼ cup quick-cooking oats
1 cup grated apple
½ cup natural peanut butter
2 eggs

NUTRITION:

Calories: 100; Fat: 3 g; Carbohydrates: 8 g; Protein: 3 g.

86 KALE CHIPS

10 minutes | 20 minutes | Easy | Golden Retriever

Ingredients:

1 head of kale, washed and dried
2 tbsp olive oil

Directions:

1. Preheat oven to 275°F.
2. Remove ribs from the kale and trim to 2" pieces. In a plastic bag, toss pieces with olive oil. Remove from the bag and spread pieces on a cookie sheet.
3. Bake kale until crisp (about 20 minutes), turning leaves half-way.

NUTRITION:

Calories: 100; Total Fat: 6 g; Total Carbs: 8 g; Protein: 5 g.

87 SPARKY'S DOGGIE TREATS

10 minutes | 17minutes | Bulldog | Easy

Directions:

1. Preheat stove to 375°F.
2. Whisk together the flour, corn flour, and cornmeal in a blending bowl.
3. Delicately oil two preparing sheets.
4. Spot the peanut butter in a microwave-safe dish, and cook in the microwave for a couple of moments all at once until the peanut butter has condensed.
5. Mix the peanut butter, water, vegetable oil, and egg into the flour blend until a solid batter structure.
6. Carry out on a floured surface and cut into treat shapes with a cutout. Spot the treats onto the pre-arranged treat sheets.
7. Prepare in the preheated stove until brilliant, 10 to 12 minutes.
8. Let the treats cool on the preparing sheets for 5 minutes before moving them to a wire rack to cool totally. Store in a sealed shut compartment.

NUTRITION:

Calories: 120; Total Fat: 8 g; Total Carbs: 10 g; Protein: 6 g.

Ingredients:

1 cup all-purpose flour
1 cup corn flour
1 cup cornmeal
½ cup smooth peanut butter
1 cup water
⅓ cup vegetable oil
1 egg

88 BANANA AND SUNFLOWER DOG COOKIES

20 minutes | 15 minutes | Shetland Sheepdog | Hard

Ingredients:

2 mashed ripe bananas
½ cup olive oil
2-2 ½ cups flour (all-purpose)
1 cup sunflower seeds, shelled and unsalted
1 tbsp powdered baking soda

Directions:

1. Combine all of the ingredients in a large mixing bowl and mix until completely combined. Add additional flour to the recipe if it's too wet; this will depend on the size of the bananas.
2. Place the bowl in the fridge for at least 30 minutes.
3. Preheat the oven to 350°F. Prepare a baking tray.
4. Make 24 small balls out of the dough. Place them on the baking tray and press down with a fork.
5. Bake for 15 minutes until golden brown. Remove from the oven and set aside to cool completely before serving or storing.

NUTRITION:

Calories: 120; Carbohydrates: 12 g; Protein: 6 g; Fat: 8 g.

89 CHIA CARROT TREATS

10 minutes   25 minutes   Bulldog   Medium

Directions:

1. Preheat your oven to 350°F (175°C).
2. Mix the dry ingredients in a bowl.
3. Add the grated carrots and slowly incorporate 1 cup of the broth to start, mixing until you reach a dough consistency that's firm enough to roll but not too wet. Depending on the absorbency of your oats or whole wheat flour, you might need to adjust by adding more broth.
4. Roll into dough.
5. Cut into desired pieces or shapes.
6. Bake for 25 minutes.

Ingredients:

2½ cups whole wheat or oats
½ lb carrots finely grated
1 cup dog-safe broth (beef or chicken)
2 tbsp chia

NUTRITION:

Calories: 120; Carbohydrates: 18 g; Fat: 2 g; Protein: 8 g.

FROZEN TREATS FOR HOT DAYS

90 CREAMY YOGURT DOG POPS

10 minutes | 0 minutes | Labrador Retriever | Medium

Directions:

1. Put your tuna can's contents in a medium bowl. Don't empty the water.
2. The tuna should be shredded into tiny bits thoroughly using a fork.
3. Yogurt and dried parsley should be added.
4. Stir everything together completely.
5. Carefully fill each space in your ice cube tray with a spoon.
6. Depending on the size of your cubes, freeze them until firm, which might take a few hours.
7. Remove from your tray just the number of cubes you will be serving right now.
8. The tray or a freezer bag with a label should be used to store any extra cubes.

Ingredients:

1 - 5 oz. can of tuna in water
2 cups of plain nonfat yogurt
1 tbsp dried parsley

NUTRITION:

Calories: 100; Carbohydrates: 8 g; Fat: 7 g; Protein: 9 g.

91 PEANUT BUTTER & JELLY FROZEN POPS

10 minutes | 0 minutes | Beagle | Hard

Ingredients:

4 cups plain yogurt, low or fat-free
1 ripe banana
1 cup of blueberries
3 tbsp peanut butter, natural and salt-free is preferred
1 tsp vanilla extract

Directions:

1. In a medium bowl, combine all the ingredients.
2. Add the contents to a blender, and mix until smooth.
3. Fill ice cube trays with the smoothie, then freeze.

NUTRITION:

Calories: 110 ; Fat: 5 g; Carbs: 12 g; Protein: 8 g

92 FROZEN FALL PUMPKIN TREATS

10 minutes   0 minutes   Greyhound   Medium

Directions:

1. All three items should be well blended.
2. Place in ice cube trays.
3. Freeze for 12 hours.
4. Place one of them into your dog bowl for a wholesome and seasonal treat.

Ingredients:

1 can 100% pure pumpkin puree
1 cup plain yogurt
½ cup peanut butter

NUTRITION:

Calories: 150; Fat: 8 g; Carbohydrates: 10 g; Protein: 8 g.

93 DOG ICE CREAM

10 minutes | 0 minutes | Rottweiler | Easy

Ingredients:

2 (6oz) containers of plain yogurt
1 tbsp Honey
½ cup of carob chips

Directions:

1. All ingredients should be well mixed in a medium basin.
2. Spoon into silicone cupcake liners or an ice cube tray.
3. Wait for 2 hours till it's firm before freezing.

NUTRITION:

Calories: 140; Carbs: 15 g; Fat: 8 g; Protein: 8 g.

94 FROZEN KING KONG

10 minutes | 0 minutes | Poodle | Easy

Directions:

1. Use half of the peanut butter to plug the small end of the KONG.
2. In a small bowl, stir banana and yogurt together, then fill KONG. Use the remaining peanut butter to plug the larger opening.
3. Serve frozen or at room temperature.

Ingredients:

1 tbsp organic unsweetened peanut butter
1 KONG
1 medium banana, mashed
1 tbsp low-fat plain yogurt

NUTRITION:

Calories: 180; Protein: 8 g; Carbs: 20 g; Fat: 10 g

95 FROSTY PAWS

10 minutes | 0 minutes | Beagle | Medium

Ingredients:

32 oz vanilla yogurt
1 large mashed banana
2 tbsp peanut butter
2 tbsp honey

Directions:

1. Blend all the ingredients in a blender and freeze in small quantities.

NUTRITION:

Calories: 200; Fat: 8 g; Protein: 10 g; Carbs: 30 g.

96   PUMPKIN ICE CREAM

10 minutes | 0 minutes | Bulldog | Easy

Directions:

1. In a blender, combine the ingredients.
2. Pour into ice cube trays and freeze.
3. Store for up to 6 months in an airtight container.

Ingredients:

1 cup pureed pumpkin
1 cup plain low-fat yogurt
½ cup unsweetened organic peanut butter

NUTRITION:

Calories: 180; Protein: 10 g; Carbs: 17 g; Fat: 10 g

97 BANANA ICE CUBES

10 minutes | 0 minutes | German Shepherd | Easy

Ingredients:

1 very ripe banana
1 Cup Water

Directions:

1. Slice the banana into pieces and put them into an ice cube tray.
2. Fill with water. The overly ripe, mushy bananas will permeate the entire ice cube with their flavor.
3. Freeze for at least 24 hours. Transfer frozen cubes to a zip-top plastic bag and keep them in the freezer for up to 2 months.

NUTRITION:

Calories: 50; Fats: 0 g; Carbs: 9 g; Protein: 2 g.

98 CARIBBEAN CANINE COOLERS

10 minutes | 0 minutes | Greyhound | Easy

Directions:

1. In a blender, combine all of the components and mix for 1-2 minutes until smooth.
2. Freeze this mixture in ice cube trays or tiny plastic tubs half-filled with it for a delicious island treat for you and your dog!

Ingredients:

3 cups yogurt (plain)
1 cup unsweetened crushed coconut flakes
1 tbsp molasses (blackstrap)
2 peeled huge mango
2 peeled bananas

NUTRITION:

Calories: 150; Carbohydrates: 18 g; Fat: 8 g; Protein: 10 g.

99 FIDO'S FROZEN FRUIT POPSICLES

10 minutes   0 minutes   Poodle   Hard

Ingredients:

1 cup cored and diced fresh fruit (not grapes or raisins)
4 cups water
1 tbsp blackstrap molasses (optional)

Directions:

1. In a large bowl, mix fruit with water and molasses, if using.
2. Freeze the mix in ice cube trays or small tubs. When frozen, store in a zip-top plastic bag in the freezer for up to 6 months.

NUTRITION:

Calories: 10; Carbohydrates: 5 g; Fat: 0 g; Protein: 0 g.

100 PEANUT BUTTER AND BANANA DOG ICE CREAM

10 minutes   0 minutes   Poodle   Easy

Directions:

1. Peel bananas and add to a blender along with yogurt and peanut butter.
2. Blend until smooth, then pour into ice cube trays.
3. Freeze and serve frozen. Freeze in an airtight container for up to 6 months.

Ingredients:

3-4 ripe bananas
4 cups low-fat plain yogurt
½ cup organic unsweetened peanut butter

NUTRITION:

Calories: 180; Fats: 8 g; Carbs: 18 g; Protein: 10 g.

DENTAL TREATS

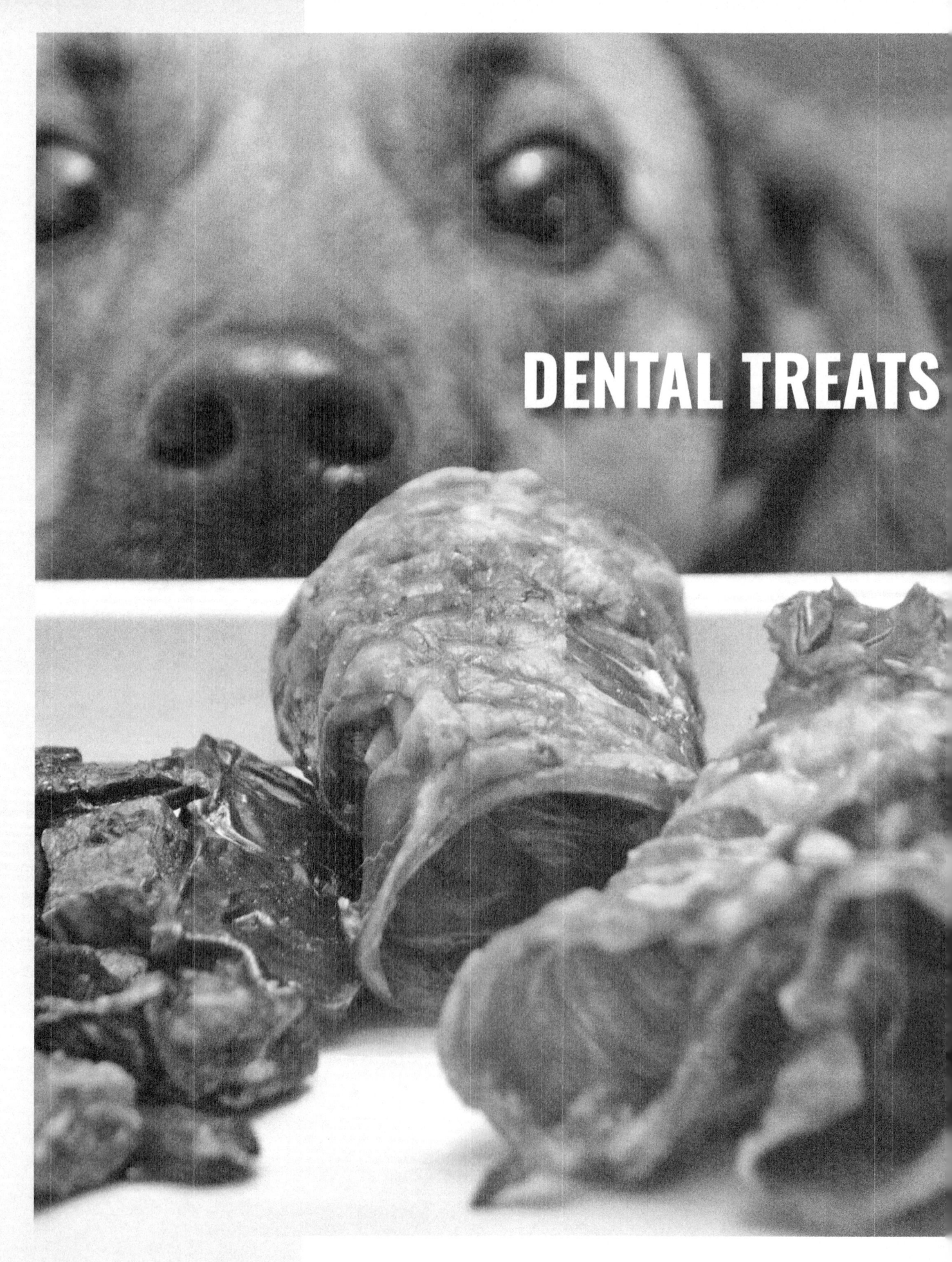

101 HOMEMADE SUNFLOWER DOG TREATS

10 minutes  | 33 minutes  | Rottweiler  | Medium

Directions:

1. Preheat the stove to 325°F. Delicately oil 2 preparing sheets.
2. Consolidate flour, sunflower seeds, oats, and flax seeds, and prepare powder in a huge bowl.
3. Mix the eggs and milk in a bowl and beat utilizing an electric blender until it all comes together. Add the mixture to the bowl with the flour and consolidate. Add chicken stock and olive oil and blend well.
4. Work batter on a floured surface for 1 to 2 minutes. Carry out batter daintily utilizing a moving pin, and cut out treats utilizing your 1 cutout. Spot on pre-arranged preparing sheets.
5. Prepare in the preheated stove until delicately caramelized, around 30 minutes. Turn the broiler off, however, pass on treats in a warm stove to fresh for 30 additional minutes.

Ingredients:

1 cup whole wheat flour
¼ cup shelled unsalted sunflower seeds
2 tbsp rolled oats
2 tbsp flax seeds
1 tsp baking powder
2 eggs
¼ cup milk
½ cup chicken broth
2 tbsp olive oil

NUTRITION:

Calories: 100; Fat: 5 g; Carbohydrates: 8 g; Protein: 6 g.

102   CHICKEN JERKY

10 minutes | 2 hours | Shetland Sheepdog | Easy

Ingredients:

2 to 4 boneless chicken breasts

Directions:

1. Preheat the oven to 200 degrees.
2. Trim excess fat off chicken.
3. Cut into ⅛ inch-thick strips.
4. Bake for 2 hours or until dry and hard.
5. Cool completely and serve as a treat.

NUTRITION:

Calories: 150; Fat: 3 g; Carbs: 0 g; Protein: 25 g.

103 BACON TREATS

10 minutes | 8 minutes | Greyhound | Easy

Directions:

1. Preheat the oven to 350°F.
2. Blend bacon and eggs.
3. Add flour. Stir in water if you need to thin the batter.
4. Smooth the batter over the baking mat and bake for eight minutes.
5. Once cooled, cut into desired treat shapes.

Ingredients:

½ package of bacon
2 eggs
1 cup flour
1 cup water

NUTRITION:

Calories: 220; Total Fat: 12 g; Total Carbs: 10 g; Protein: 10 g.

104 PUMPKIN TURMERIC TREATS

10 minutes | 3 hours | Beagle | Medium

Ingredients:

1 lb Ground venison
1 cup oats
1 can organic pumpkin puree
75-100 mg of turmeric per 5 lb bodyweight
2 eggs
1 cup ground flax seed

Directions:

1. Set the temperature of the oven to 250°F and prepare the food.
2. Gather the ingredients and mix them.
3. Cut 45 pieces of dough out of it.
4. Bake for about three hours.
5. One goodie every day should be given.

NUTRITION:

Calories: 100; Fats: 4 g; Carbs: 5 g; Protein: 5 g

105 LIVER LOGS

20 minutes | 10 minutes | Shetland Sheepdog | Hard

Directions:

1. Remove the cream cheese from the refrigerator and let it soften before preparing the liver.
2. In a large skillet, heat the oil over medium-high heat. Toss in the liver and cook until it is well done. Remove the liver from the heat, then split it as much as possible with a fork.
3. Combine cream cheese and chicken livers in a mixing dish with a fork or hand mixer. Stir until the liver is smooth.
4. Each treat consists of one celery stalk (no need to trim off the leaves). Celery should be washed and the ends trimmed.
5. Fill with cream cheese-liver mixture by forking it in. Keep refrigerated for up to three days.

Ingredients:

8 oz cream cheese (220 g)
2 tbsp olive oil
½ lb chicken liver, washed
1 celery head

NUTRITION:

Calories: 140; Fats: 8 g; Carbs: 4 g; Protein: 10 g.

CHAPTER 7
SHOPPING LIST

Cooking your dog treats and/or meals can be a money-saver—as long as you think ahead and shop with a plan. Here are some tips for buying ingredients inexpensively:

Look for "last chance" meats, fruits, and vegetables. Although they're still safe to eat, these foods that are close to their expiration dates are often deeply discounted at grocery stores for a fast sale. In the case of fruits and vegetables, their ripe or slightly overripe state may make them less palatable to humans, but they'll be more easily digested by your dog.

Check local farmers' markets for bruised or slightly damaged fruits and vegetables. Locally grown produce isn't just an eco-friendly choice but a great way to save money and get food at the peak of freshness. Buying bruised produce can be a great way to save on dog meal ingredients; many farmers will even give them away, especially if you're making another purchase.

Shopping List for Your Dog

Meat and Animal Products

These should always make up at least half of the diet. Raw diets for dogs can be high in fat, which leads to obesity. Another hazard of diets that are too high in fat is that when restricting how much a dog is given to control weight, the dog may develop a deficiency for some required nutrients. Unless you provide your dog with regular, intense exercise, then you should use lean meats with no more than 10% fat, remove the skin from poultry, and cut off any separable fat. It is best to feed dark meat poultry rather than breast meat; unless your dog needs a very low-fat diet.

Raw Meaty Bones

If you feed with bony parts like chicken necks and back, then you should trend to the lower end of the range. If you use meatier parts like the thighs, then you can use more. You should also never feed cooked bones.

Fish

This is a good source of Vitamin D, which needs to be supplemented. Some good choices are canned fish with bones like sardines, jack mackerel, and pink salmon. You should remove the bones from the fish you cook yourself and never feed your dog raw fish. You can feed it with small amounts of fish each day, or you can feed it in larger amounts once or twice a week. The total amount you feed shouldn't exceed one ounce of fish per pound of other meats.

Organs

In this particular category, the liver should comprise around 5%, which is equal to one ounce of

173

liver for every pound of other animal products. The most nutritious option is beef liver, but you should include other liver types occasionally as well. You should feed your dog small amounts of liver each day or every other day rather than feeding a larger portion of liver less often.

Eggs

These are a highly nutritious addition to any diet. Dogs who weigh about twenty pounds can have a whole egg each day, but smaller dogs should get less.

Dairy

Most dogs tolerate plain yogurt and kefir well. Some other good options are cottage and ricotta cheeses. However, you should limit other forms of cheese since they are high in fat.

Starchy Vegetables

Vegetables such as potatoes, sweet potatoes, and winter squashes along with legumes provide carbohydrate calories that can help reduce the cost of a homemade food diet while keeping weight on dogs who are underweight and/or highly active. For overweight dogs, the quantities should be limited. To be digestible, you need to cook starchy vegetables.

Non-Starchy and Leafy Green Vegetables

These vegetables are low in calories and can be added as much as you like. Just keep in mind that too much of these vegetables can cause gas. In addition, raw, cruciferous vegetables such as broccoli and cauliflower can intentionally suppress thyroid function. Raw vegetables need to be pureed in a food processor, blender, or juicer so that the dog can digest them properly. Whole raw vegetables aren't harmful and can even be fed as treats.

Grains

This category is controversial since it can cause inflammation as a result of allergies, arthritis, or inflammatory bowel disease (IBD). Some grains also contain gluten which can cause digestive problems in some dogs. Most dogs will do fine with grains, and this can help reduce the cost of feeding a homemade diet.

Grains and starchy vegetables shouldn't make up any more than half a diet. Some good grain choices are oatmeal, brown rice, quinoa, barley, and pasta. You can use white rice to settle an upset stomach. However, white rice is low in nutrition and shouldn't make up a large portion of the diet. Ensure all grains you use are well cooked.

Pork

Pork is a good meat source for dogs since it is highly digestible protein full of amino acids. However, it does contain more calories per pound than other meats. Pork is less likely to cause allergic reactions compared to other protein sources for dogs.

Quinoa

This is okay for dogs and is found in some high-quality dry dog foods. It has a strong nutritional profile that makes it a great alternative to corn, wheat, and soy.

Salmon

Salmon is a great option for dogs. Fully cooked salmon is a great source of protein, good fats, and amino acids. It will boost your dog's immune system while promoting joint and brain health. Just avoid raw or undercooked salmon since it can contain parasites that make dogs sick with the symptoms of vomiting, diarrhea, dehydration, and even death in extreme cases.

Shrimp

This is okay now and then for your dog. Just ensure they are fully cooked and remove the shell, tail, head, and legs. Shrimp are a great source of antioxidants, Vitamin B12, and phosphorus; while also being low in fat, calories, and carbohydrates.

Tuna

Tuna is okay in moderation when cooked. Fresh tuna is a great source of Omega-3 fatty acids that can benefit the eyes and heart. It is best to limit the consumption of canned tuna due to its potential mercury and sodium content. Some canned tuna and juice occasionally is fine, just make sure it is prepared in water and oil without any added spices.

Turkey

Turkey is a good meat source for dogs, but you need to make sure you remove excess fat and skin from the meat first. You should also check for bones since poultry bones can splinter when ingested and cause a blockage or tear in the intestines. You also should avoid feeding any turkey meat that has excessive salt, seasonings, or spices.

Blueberries

This superfood is okay for dogs and is high in antioxidants that can help prevent cell damage. They also contain fiber and phytochemicals. This can be a great alternative to store-bought treats for your dog when training.

Cantaloupe

This is safe for dogs since it is full of nutrients, low in calories, and a great source of fiber and water. However, it is high in sugar so, it should be given in moderation; especially for dogs who are overweight or diagnosed with diabetes.

Cranberries

These are safe in both fresh and dried forms as long as they are fed in small quantities. Whether or not dogs will like the tart flavor is another issue. Just feed in moderation since too much can cause stomach upset.

Cucumbers

These are a good option, especially for overweight dogs, since they have little to no carbohydrates, fats, and oils. In addition, they can help boost energy levels. They are a good source of Vitamins K, C, and B1, along with potassium, copper, magnesium, and biotin.

Pears

These are a great source of copper, Vitamin C, and K, and fiber for dogs. Make sure you cut them into chunks and remove the pits and seeds first. Also, avoid canned pears that can be high in sugar.

Pineapple

A few chunks of pineapple make a sweet treat for dogs as long as you remove the outside peel and crown first. This fruit contains vitamins, minerals, and fiber. It also contains bromelain, an enzyme that will make it easier for your dog to absorb proteins.

Raspberries

In moderation, these are good for dogs. They contain antioxidants while being low in sugar and calories while being high in fiber, manganese, and Vitamin C. The anti-inflammatory properties of raspberries are great for senior dogs to help with aging joints. However, raspberries do contain a small amount of xylitol, so they should only be fed less than a cup at a time.

Strawberries

These are a great source of fiber and Vitamin C for dogs. Additionally, within them lies an enzyme that has the potential to naturally enhance the whiteness of your canine companion's teeth. Just give them in moderation because of their sugar content.

Tomatoes

You shouldn't feed these to your dog. While the ripe fruit is considered safe, the green parts of a tomato plant contain a toxin called solanine. While a dog needs to ingest a large part of the plant to become sick, it is best to avoid tomatoes entirely because of the risk.

Watermelon

This is okay for dogs as long as you remove the rind and seeds first since they can cause intestinal blockage. Watermelon is a good source of vitamins A, B6, and C along with potassium. Since watermelon is 92 percent water, it is a great way to help keep dogs hydrated as well.

Brussels Sprouts

These are high in nutrients and antioxidants for both humans and dogs. Just make sure you don't overfeed them since they can cause gas. The same applies to cabbage.

Carrots

Carrots are a great low-calorie snack for dogs and contain a good amount of fiber and beta-carotene that leads to the production of Vitamin A. Also, crunching on carrots is a great source for cleaning a dog's teeth.

Celery

You can feed this to dogs since it contains nut[rients] needed to promote a healthy heart and c[an] even help fight cancer. It is a good source of [vi]tamins A, B, and C. Celery can also help fresh[en] the breath.

Corn

This is a common ingredient in dog food. How[ev]er, you should use the corn cob cautiou[sly] since it can be difficult to digest and is prone [to] intestinal blockage.

Green Beans

All types of green beans are safe for dogs to e[at] as long as you make sure they are plain. Th[ey] contain several important vitamins and miner[als] while being full of fiber and low in calories. Ma[ke] sure you choose a low-salt or no-salt optio[n] feeding canned green beans.

Peas

All types of peas are okay for dogs to eat. The[re] are several vitamins and minerals in peas. Th[ey] are also high in fiber and protein. Fresh or froz[en] peas are best, but avoid peas that contain add[ed] sodium.

Spinach

This is good for dogs, but it isn't a top vegetab[le] you'll want to use in a homemade diet. Spina[ch] is high in oxalic acid, which can block the absor[p]tion of calcium and can eventually lead to k[id]ney damage. While a dog will need to eat a lar[ge] amount of spinach to create a problem, it is like[ly] best to choose other vegetables.

CHAPTER 8
CONVERSION TABLES

	U.S. STANDARD	U.S. STANDARD (OUNCES)	METRIC (APPROXIMATE)		
VOLUME EQUIVALENTS (LIQUID)	2 tbsps	1 fl. oz.	30 mL		
	¼ cup	2 fl. oz.	60 mL		
	½ cup	4 fl. oz.	120 mL		
	1 cup	8 fl. oz.	240 mL		
	1½ cups	12 fl. oz.	355 mL		
	2 cups or 1 pint	16 fl. oz.	475 mL		
	4 cups or 1 quart	32 fl. oz.	1 L		
	1 gallon	128 fl. oz.	4 L		
VOLUME EQUIVALENTS (DRY)	⅛ tsp		0.5 mL		
	¼ tsp		1 mL		
	½ tsp		2 mL		
	¾ tsp		4 mL		
	1 tsp		5 mL		
	1 tbsp		15 mL		
	¼ cup		59 mL		
	⅓ cup		79 mL		
	½ cup		118 mL		
	⅔ cup		156 mL		
	¾ cup		177 mL		
	1 cup		235 mL		
	2 cups or 1 pint		475 mL		
	3 cups		700 mL		
	4 cups or 1 quart		1 L		
	½ gallon		2 L		
	1 gallon		4 L		
WEIGHT EQUIVALENTS		½ ounce		15 g	
		1 ounce		30 g	
		2 ounces		60 g	
		4 ounces		115 g	
		8 ounces		225 g	
		12 ounces		340 g	
		16 ounces or 1 pound		455 g	

	FAHRENHEIT (F)	CELSIUS (C) (APPROXIMATE)
OVEN TEMPERATURES	250°F	120°C
	300°F	150°C
	325°F	180°C
	375°F	190°C
	400°F	200°C
	425°F	220°C
	450°F	230°C

Thank you for coming this far!
Your opinion is extremely important!
Scan the QR code, leave a review and download your free BONUS!

INDEX

A

Almond and Banana Treats	142
Appetizing Sea Food	99
Apple Cheddar Biscuits	145

B

Bacon Gravy	60
Bacon Treats	169
Baked Eggs Muffins	81
Banana and Sunflower Dog Cookies	152
Banana Ice Cubes	162
Basic Baked Chicken Treats	144
Basic Chicken With Rice	104
Bean Soup	132
Beef and Sweet Potato Stew	87
Beef Dinner Delight	130
Beef Fried Rice	90
Beef Stew	91
Birthday Blueberry Cupcakes	121
Birthday Bones	122
Brothsicles	118

C

Cabbage Beefy salad	89
Caribbean Canine Coolers	163
Carob Dog Biscuits	143
Cheese Biscuits	61
Cheesy Eggs and Rice	76
Chia Carrot Treats	153
Chia Seed Oatmeal	82
Chicken and Cheese Meal	108
Chicken and Vegetable Medley	109
Chicken Casserole	105
Chicken Cookies	129
Chicken Jerky	168
Chicken Risotto	103
Chicken & Sweet Potato	112
Chicken Thighs and Tabbouleh	107
Chickpea Stew	135

Chuck and Barley Stew	57
Cottage Cheese Breakfast	80
Creamy Yogurt Dog Pops	155
Crunchy Apple Cupcakes	62

D

Dehydrated Sweet Potato Chews	70
Dog 158	
Doggie Bagels	63
Doggy Cookies	65

E

Easy Slow Beef and Beans	114

F

Fido's Frozen Fruit Popsicles	164
Fishermen's Eggs	83
Fish Homestyle Dinner	96
Frosty Paws	160
Frozen Fall Pumpkin Treats	157
Frozen King	159
Fruity Chicken Soup	133

G

Ground Beef Homestyle Dinner	88
Ground Meat Loaf	86

H

Halloween Chicken Fingers	126
Homemade Breakfast for Dogs	74
Homemade Chicken Broth	102
Homemade Dog French Omelet	77
Homemade Dog Treats	149
Homemade Sunflower Dog Treats	167

K

Kale Chips	150

L

Liver Corn Bread	75
Liver Gravy	64
Liver Logs	171

M

Max and Penny's Spinach	134

P

Pampered Pooch Rice and Lamb Casserole	55
Parsley Fish & Oregano	93
Peanut Butter and Banana Dog Biscuits	141
Peanut Butter and Banana Dog Ice Cream	165
Peanut Butter & Jelly Frozen Pops	156
Peanut Butter Oatmeal	78
Peanut Butter Treats	146
Potato Cranberry Christmas Cookies	125
Poultry Palooza	106
Pumpkin-Apple Dog Treats	139
Pumpkin Balls	136
Pumpkin & Berry Oatmeal	79
Pumpkin Ice Cream	161
Pumpkin Rice	137
Pumpkin Treats	147
Pumpkin Turmeric Treats	170

Q

Quick and Easy Homemade Dog Treat	140

R

Raw Veggie and Fruit Dog Treat	68
Raw Veggie Cupcakes	67
Rice and Salmon	94
Rice With Beef and Fish	58

S

Salmon and Spinach Hash	98
Salmon Balls	97
Senior Chicken Dinner	131
Senior Dogs Chili	128
Slow Beef and Turkey	115
Slow Chicken	117
Slow-Cooked Chicken and Barley	116
South Pacific Hot Dogs	54
Sparky's Doggie Treats	151
Spinach Omelet	73
Stomach Friendly Kibble	56
Sweet Potato Potstickers	124

T

Tapioca and Tofu	71
Tuna Balls	100
Tuna Casserole	69
Turkey and Vegetables	111
Turkey Gravy	110
Turmeric Beef	85

V

Valentine Hearts	123
Valentine's Day Red Bell Pepper Cookies	120
Vegetable/Fish Patties	95

Printed in Great Britain
by Amazon